The Wondrous Adventures
of
Saint Francis of Assisi

TRICIA GRAY

ILLUSTRATIONS BY VICKI SHUCK

ST. ANTHONY MESSENGER PRESS

Cincinnati, Ohio

For the eminent Franciscan scholar, Brother Raphael Brown, S.F.O. (rest in peace), whose encouragement inspired me to adapt these wonderful stories for readers in our modern age and all ages to come, for Father Claude Francis Ignatius, S.C.S.T., who never let me give up, and for Monsignor Tullio Andreatta, K.H.S., whose spiritual support and example help me day by day to do all for the glory of the Lord Jesus Christ. Deo Gratias!

Scripture citations are taken from the *New Revised Standard Version Bible*, copyright ©1989 by the Division of Christian Education of the National Council of Churches of Christ in the U.S.A. and used by permission.

Most of the tales herein are adapted from stories in *Francis of Assisi: Early Documents, Volume I: The Saint, Volume II: The Founder an Volume III: The Prophet*, edited by Regis J. Armstrong, O.F.M. CAP., J. A. Wayne Hellmann, O.F.M. Conv., and William J. Short, O.F.M., published by New City Press, in 1999, 2000 and 2001. Three of the tales, "The Virtue of Fear," "The Reward of the Ploughed Field" and "The Mighty Power of Prayer," are adapted from stories in "A New Fioretti: A Collection of Early Stories about Saint Francis of Assisi" from *English Omnibus of the Sources for the Life of St. Francis, Fourth Revised Edition*, edited by Marion A. Habig, published by Franciscan Press in 1991.

Cover and book design by Mark Sullivan
Illustrations by Vicki Shuck

Library of Congress Cataloging-in-Publication Data

Gray, Tricia.
  The wondrous adventures of Saint Francis of Assisi / Tricia Gray.
     v. cm.
Summary: Recounts various stories about how St. Francis influenced everyone he met to lead a better life.
Contents: The three murderous robbers -- The miserable leper -- The hail and the ravenous wolves -- Brother Masseo's wild whirling -- The multiplication of the grapes -- The virtue of fear -- The reward of the ploughed field -- The wicked wolf of Gubbio -- The stricken oxen -- The obedient birds -- The mighty power of prayer -- The thirsty peasant -- John the Simple -- The money snake -- Miracles of the manger.
  ISBN 0-86716-480-8 (pbk.)
  1. Francis, of Assisi, Saint, 1182-1226--Juvenile literature. 2. Christian saints--Italy--Assisi--Biography--Juvenile literature. 3. Assisi (Italy)--Biography--Juvenile literature. [1. Francis, of Assisi, Saint, 1182-1226. 2. Saints.] I. Title.
  BX4700.F69 G73 2003
  271'.302--dc21

ISBN 0-86716-480-8
Copyright ©2003, Tricia Gray
All rights reserved.
Published by St. Anthony Messenger Press
www.AmericanCatholic.org
Printed in the U.S.A.

Contents

A long time

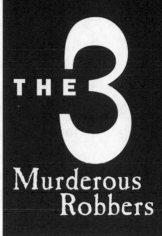

THE 3 Murderous Robbers

ago there lived a young man in Assisi, Italy, called Francis. He had everything—family, friends, money and comfort. But it wasn't enough! One day God spoke to Francis, filling up the empty space. After that, nothing was the same!

Francis was already cheerful, kind and generous. But suddenly he wanted to use his goodness to please God. So he began traveling from place to place, praying and speaking about God. His love for God was so amazing people wanted to be like him!

Soon, many men were following his instructions. These men believed that if they lived like Francis, they would become like him. And because they tried, they began to love God more. This was the beginning of Francis' religious brotherhood. In time, they had to have many houses for all those following Francis' way.

One of the little houses was in a village called Monte Casale. It was there that Brother Francis received a young man into the brotherhood and gave him the name "Brother Angelo."

After a while, Brother Angelo was appointed the brother in charge of the house. At the time there were three murderous robbers living in the area. They had committed so many crimes the people were terrified to walk on the roads by day or by night.

One bright spring day the robbers came to Monte Casale. They banged noisily on the door of the brothers' house, but there was no answer. Yelling angrily, they tried to scare someone into opening the door.

"Open up! We're hungry," the largest of the robbers bellowed. He glared furiously at the little window in the door. The shutter was closed tight and did not budge.

"No one will answer," the second robber growled. He rubbed a long scar on his cheek, scratching his matted hair.

"We'll have to burn the place down," the third one hissed through broken yellow teeth, fingering his long knife.

Suddenly, the little window was whipped open and the round cupid-like face of Brother Angelo filled the space. "What do you want?" he asked with a start, recognizing them immediately. They were the three murderous robbers who had been tormenting the people of the area.

"Food, imbecile! We want food. Didn't you hear me yelling? Are you deaf as well as stupid?" the huge robber bellowed back, his bearded face flushing.

Brother Angelo stared for a long moment. Anger slowly turned his pale face beet red. "How dare you come here asking for something to eat? You robbers and murderers aren't even ashamed of the crimes you commit. Then you have the nerve to try to eat up what we poor brothers bring home by the grace of God! You do not even deserve to walk on the earth God created! You have no respect for man or beast or the Holy God who created you. Get out of here and never come back!" he roared, hitting the door with his doubled fist. Then he quickly slammed the wooden shutter over the window. Hurriedly, he pulled a thick bar into place to keep the angry robbers out. None too soon! The sound of their fists beating furiously on the door echoed back to him.

Finally, they saw they could not get in. They left,

yelling curses and threats all the way down the road.

That same day, Brother Francis returned after many hours of preaching the holy gospel of Jesus. He brought a very large jug of fine wine and a thick hot loaf of freshly baked bread for the brothers' dinner.

Kneeling in front of Brother Francis, Brother Angelo quickly told him about the visit of the robbers. His anger was gone. His face was very pale and his hands were still shaking. All that remained was regret.

Brother Francis stared down at the thin brother, the jug of wine in one hand and the loaf of bread in the other. His gaunt bearded face grew sad. His dark liquid eyes filled with tears, but for a moment there was a glint of anger in the inky interior of his gaze. Straightening his thin shoulders, he spoke.

"You were very cruel, Brother Angelo," said Brother Francis. "We cannot bring men to love the Lord by angrily scolding them or upbraiding them for their wrongdoings. They see only themselves in that kind of behavior. They would not see a need to change if they thought we were all like them." He paused, slowly shaking his head.

"Sinners are led to God through meekness and gentleness," he continued, "by showing them we are willing to love them, as Jesus did." Brother Francis' dark eyes shone as if he were looking into the face of Jesus at that very moment!

Brother Angelo hung his head, suddenly seeing how wrong he had been.

Brother Francis' voice grew gentle when he saw Brother Angelo's head droop. "Remember, Brother Angelo," he said, "our Master told us in his Gospels that the doctor is not needed by those who are well, but by the sick. He did not come to call the just to repentance but the sinner."

"I, too, am a sinner. I have sinned against God and those three men," Brother Angelo whispered, not even able to look at Brother Francis.

Brother Francis' heart ached for the young brother. Still, he compressed his thin lips and forced himself to remain very stern. Brother Francis knew Brother Angelo had to learn to walk the gospel way and that he would only learn by actually doing what Jesus would do.

"Yes, we are all sinners, Brother," said Brother Francis. "Now, I command you under holy obedience to take this jug of wine and loaf of bread. Search carefully for the robbers. Search the mountains, the hills, the valleys and the dells. When you find them, offer them all of this bread and wine for me, in the name of Jesus. Kneel down in front of them. Then, humbly beg their forgiveness for the sin of cruelty." Brother Francis paused, seeing the young brother trembling with fear at what he had to do.

"Then ask them, my brother," Francis went on, "for me, in Jesus' name, to stop doing the evil things they have been doing. Ask them to fear God. Ask them to remember he will be the one to open either heaven or hell to them when they die. And ask them never to offend God and their neighbors again. Tell them, if they agree to do this, I will give them food and drink the rest of their lives. Finally, when you have done all of this, come back here." Brother Francis waited, seeing Brother Angelo had stopped trembling.

Brother Angelo lifted his head, his eyes full of a beautiful compassion. Tears ran down his cheeks as he nodded in obedience.

So Brother Angelo left Monte Casale and began to search the mountains, the hills, the valleys and the dells for the three murderous robbers.

While Brother Angelo was searching, Brother Francis knelt down on the hard stones in front of the crucifix of Jesus. He began to pray that the hearts of the murderous robbers would soften. He prayed that they would begin to fear God enough to repent and change their ways.

Brother Angelo tramped steadily down the road. He had seen many people. All of them had a similar response when he asked where the murderous robbers could be found. They said, "Follow the road, Brother. They'll find you!"

Turning a bend in the road, Brother Angelo came upon a farmer sitting dejectedly in his field. He looked very tired and sad. His hat shaded his tearful face. So Brother Angelo stopped to cheer him up and ask directions.

"Why are you so downcast on such a beautiful day, sir?" Brother Angelo asked and smiled, inhaling the sweet smell of cut hay.

"Oh, Brother," the farmer sighed, wiping his eyes on his shirtsleeve, "not long ago three robbers came and stole all the money I had made from selling my eggs and vegetables." Shaking his head, he stared at his hands in his lap. "I needed that money to buy medicine for my wife," he said, "and now I don't know what to do."

"I am so sorry," Brother Angelo said slowly. Reaching into his sack, he brought out the coin he had been given for his journey. "Here, take this coin and go buy your medicine," he said. Pressing the coin into the man's hand, he waited. Brother Angelo wanted to give the farmer the jug of wine and the bread, too, but he knew he was bound by holy obedience to give it to the three murderous robbers.

The farmer smiled, at once more cheerful. Standing up, he patted Brother Angelo on the back. "Thank you, Brother," he said. "Now you be careful on this road because the robbers may not have gone too far. They have killed many men."

That was not what Brother Angelo wanted to hear, but, forcing a smile, he turned back to his journey. After a while, he came down into the valley. He could see smoke billowing from a burning house by the road. Flames leapt high into the air. Wood crackled and crashed as it fell burning to the ground. A small crowd of people stood back, helplessly watching the house turning to charred rubble.

"What happened?" Brother Angelo asked, hurrying up to the nearest man, who was leaning on a long crutch.

"The robbers," the man said, as his broad, soot-smeared face grew red with anger. "They could get no food here so they killed the owner and burned his house."

Brother Angelo stared in disbelief, his mouth gaping. 'What am I getting myself into?' he thought, perspiration beading his forehead. Reluctantly, he turned back to the road, thinking, 'Surely they will kill me, too!'

Swallowing painfully over the lump in his throat, he went on, his heart heavy with fear as his teeth chattered noisily. "Please," he prayed, "give me the courage to carry out my mission for the love of Jesus."

Walking steadily through a stand of trees into a small dell, Brother Angelo paused in a shaded glen. He heard the soft sound of crying close by. Brushing back his perspiration-dampened hair, he peered into the shadows. "Hello?" he whispered, his blue eyes wide with fear. And then, seeing a small boy leaning against the trunk of a thick tree, he said louder, "Why are you crying, boy?"

The boy jumped. "You frightened me, Brother," said the boy, looking up at him. Then the boy peered this way and that, as if looking for someone else.

That was when Brother Angelo noticed the little dog

lying in the boy's lap. Its wiry fur was matted with blood.

"Who did this?" asked Brother Angelo, hurrying to the boy and putting down his sack. The little terrier whimpered.

"Three robbers came," the boy sniffed, stroking his dog's head. Slowly he wiped his nose on his sleeve. "They took my bread and cheese," he went on, "and one of them cut Doggy with his long knife because he wouldn't stop barking at him." Covering his face, the boy sobbed loudly into his hands.

"Poor Doggy," Brother Angelo murmured. "Don't cry, child," he said, and, patting the boy's arm, he opened his bag. Taking out his water gourd and some medicine he squatted down. Carefully he tore a little strip of linen from the cloth the bread was wrapped in. After cleaning the wound he sprinkled some medicine powder on it. Then he gently bandaged it. "Now, you give Doggy some water and carry him home so he can be warm." Brother Angelo smiled at the boy.

"Will he be all right?" the boy asked, raising his tear-stained face to Brother Angelo, his big dark eyes hopeful.

"He'll be all right," Brother Angelo smiled again. "Say a little prayer for him, too. Okay?"

"Okay," said the boy. Getting up with Doggy in his arms, the boy shuffled his bare feet. Suddenly he was very nervous. "I have nothing to pay you with," he said softly.

"You don't need to pay me!" Brother Angelo laughed, "because I did it for the love of Jesus."

"Thank you!" the boy said and smiled, turning away. Hurrying off, he turned once to wave.

Waving back, Brother Angelo picked up his things. Once again he continued his search. What kind of men were these robbers? How could they hurt a child's dog?

Surely, their hearts were hard as stone. Shuddering, Brother Angelo prayed even more fervently to be able to do what Jesus would do when he came face to face with these men. Could he? Would he? His steps faltered. And then he remembered the beautiful look in Brother Francis' eyes as he seemed to be looking at the face of Jesus.

"I can do it, with your help, Lord," Brother Angelo said, suddenly humbled.

Finally, Brother Angelo found the cave the robbers were using for a home. He quietly followed the path up the hill. Stopping in his tracks, he trembled at the sound of the robbers quarreling. "Run!" his heart said. "Holy obedience!" his head said, and so he stayed.

"Okay," he whispered, his breath shallow with fear. "Hello?" he called loudly, and clutched the jug of wine more tightly. Then he whispered another prayer for courage.

"Who is that?" one of the robbers bellowed, charging out with a club in one hand.

"It must be the law!" another robber leapt into the light swinging his long knife.

"Wait!" Brother Angelo cried.

The last robber loomed in the shadows of the dark cave. Holding up his enormous fists like huge hammers, he glared at Brother Angelo. "Who are you and what do you want?" he demanded.

For a moment, Brother Angelo's head began to spin. His heart thumped wildly in his chest. He swayed unsteadily, sure he would faint from fear.

"I asked you a question!" the largest robber roared.

"I . . . I . . . I am Brother Angelo," Brother Angelo squeaked.

"Brother Angelo?" the second robber asked, and

thumped the club against a grimy palm. "He is the brother who treated us so foully!" he sneered, the long scar on his cheek livid.

"So!" the robber with the long knife grinned, his broken yellow teeth making him look more menacing. "You have a lot of guts coming here."

And as the robbers closed in on him, Brother Angelo began to pray, because he knew if he didn't pray his courage would fail him and he would run.

He heard their words accusing him of his sins. Then he remembered Brother Francis. As he prayed, the fear grew smaller in him. He began to speak as the robbers surrounded him. "Brothers, you are right," he said, dropping his gaze in shame. "I treated you cruelly. I sinned grievously against you and God. Now I bring food and wine. Please accept them."

For a moment, the largest robber stared at Brother Angelo as if he were speaking another language. Then he turned, staring at his companions.

"Give me that wine," the robber with the knife said as he grabbed the jug of wine and hurried back into the cave.

The second robber lifted his club as though he would hit the brother, but Brother Angelo did not cower.

"Please, brother," Brother Angelo said softly, "take this loaf of bread."

Glancing at the bread and then the largest robber, the second robber lowered his club.

The largest robber snatched the bread and dragged Brother Angelo into the cave. "I should crush your throat right now," he said in a growl. "Why did you follow us?"

Praying silently, Brother Angelo inhaled a deep breath. "I came to beg you to forgive me for my cruel treatment of you," he said.

"To beg us?" the huge robber burst into loud laughter.

Brother Angelo's face burned with shame.

The three robbers divided the bread and began to devour it. Slurping wine from wooden cups, they watched Brother Angelo. It was as if they thought he would try to run away.

But the longer he stayed and the more he prayed, the less fear blinded Brother Angelo. He was no longer afraid of what the robbers would do to him. He began to feel a deep sadness for them, knowing how unhappy they were in their sins.

Looking more like an angel than a man, Brother Angelo knelt. Raising his arms to the robbers, he said, "Please, brothers, I beg you in the name of Jesus and on behalf of Brother Francis, to stop doing the evil things you have been doing."

The robbers froze. Hands halfway to their mouths, they stared at him. But Brother Angelo went on.

"I beg you to stop because you fear God, fear him because he is the one who will open heaven or hell to you when you die," said Brother Angelo. He lowered his arms and joined his hands in prayer. "I beg you and I pray you will never offend God and your neighbor again."

The robbers continued to stare. The candle on their crude wooden table suddenly seemed dim. The shining cupid-like face of Brother Angelo shone in the darkness beseechingly.

"And if you agree to do this," said Brother Angelo, "Brother Francis will give you food and drink the rest of your lives." Closing his eyes, Brother Angelo grew very quiet. His fear was gone. He could feel the warmth of Jesus' love surrounding him.

"Good bread," the biggest robber grunted, clearing his

throat. Suddenly he wanted to talk. He could feel a strange warmth from Brother Angelo and talking made him more comfortable.

"Yes, it is good bread and fine wine," the second robber agreed, belching loudly. He inhaled uneasily, looking at his companions one by one. Then he looked back at Brother Angelo, shuddering.

"I wonder what horrible tortures God is going to let the devil deal out to us for all the misery and evil we've done," the third robber said, gulping wine. He, too, was unable to stop staring at the brother's shining face.

The biggest robber shivered as a chill raced up his back. He stared uncomfortably at the little brother. "I don't know. If we had any fear of God, we wouldn't rob and murder," he said, chewing his bread vigorously.

"I cannot understand what made this brother come after us like this," the second robber said. "He may have been angry, but everything he said was true."

"It was true all right," the third robber admitted, "but he was shaking like a leaf when he first got here. Then ... he ... he ... wasn't scared at all."

"He called us 'brothers,'" the second robber said, swallowing a lump in his throat.

"He must be a very holy man, to trust God and come all the way out here alone to do what he did," said the third robber, narrowing his eyes. He tipped his head at Brother Angelo, who was still kneeling, his lips moving in prayer, his eyes still closed. Light seemed to surround him.

"This Brother Francis promised to feed us if we stop robbing," the first robber said aloud. He turned his cup of wine, watching the light play on the ruby red liquid.

"And if we stop killing," the third robber said in a quiet voice, fingering his long knife.

"What if we did go and ask forgiveness of God?" the first robber asked suddenly. "Would God be as gentle or as merciful as this Brother Francis?"

"After all we've done? I don't think we'll be able to get mercy from God," the second robber said, hurriedly tearing off another hunk of bread.

"But there is . . . there is still hell . . ." The first robber's big shoulders shuddered. It was as if he had seen a glimpse of what was in store for him.

The three robbers turned and looked at Brother Angelo.

"God is mercy and kindness," Brother Angelo said slowly. "We are made in his image so we can show mercy and kindness. But our mercy is only a small measure of what he is able to offer." Opening his eyes he looked into the face of each of the robbers. "Jesus will show those who repent the full measure of his divine mercy and unfathomable kindness."

"All right!" the third robber said and jumped to his feet. "Let's go talk to this Brother Francis. If he, too, gives us hope of being forgiven, we'll do it! If he thinks God will be merciful, we'll do whatever he commands us!"

"Yes!" the second robber cried. "Then we'll be free of the threat of hell!"

The first robber rose menacingly to his full height, his face becoming a glowering mask. Then slowly his expression changed. "Come on then, little brother," he said to Brother Angelo, "show us the way back."

Brother Francis welcomed them to the brothers' house in Monte Casale. With a radiant smile and great words of holy consolation he embraced them. He took the robbers inside and spoke so well about God's mercy they were astonished. He promised them, if they repented, they would be forgiven by the Lord Jesus. He showed them with his gentle, kind words and actions how God's mercy is greater than all our sins. He told them how Jesus came into the world to redeem sinners, not to condemn them.

One by one, the murderous robbers fell to their knees. Their hearts were so deeply touched they repented all their sins. And, to everyone's surprise, they asked to be received as brothers in Brother Francis' religious order!

After proper instruction, they were gladly admitted. Then they prayerfully, with humbled hearts, lived out the remainder of their lives as faithful followers of Jesus Christ, in Brother Francis' Way.

"Someone!"

The leper's voice boomed off the walls of the house of mercy the little brothers of Brother Francis ran. "You imbeciles, come here!"

Still no one came.

THE Miserable Leper

"Listen, Brother Antonio, I do understand that good Brother Francis has commanded us, out of holy obedience, to care for the sick, to care for the dying and to care for the poor. I understand that!" Brother Thomas was nearly blue in the face explaining. "But I won't go!"

"You have to go, Brother Thomas." Brother Antonio wrung his hands, a deep frown making his face look even longer than it was. "I went every day last week. Brother Edward the week before!"

"Somebody!" Again the leper in the last room at the end of the hall yelled. The plates rattled, the walls seemed to tremble. "Get your stupid, incompetent . . . !" He went on to describe body parts that should not be spoken about in terrible, filthy words.

Brother Thomas crossed his arms over his broad chest. "No! I won't go!" he said.

"Please." Brother Antonio stopped trying to make Brother Thomas be obedient. Instead he began to beg. "Please, please, please . . ." He clasped his hands and dropped to one knee. "We all have to take turns. Even if he is . . . unpleasant."

"Unpleasant!" Brother Thomas's arms flew open, his hands making fists. "He is miserable . . . horrible . . . hideous. I can't stand to be in the same room with him.

Not only is his body rotting and stinks to high heaven, his mouth is even worse." Brother Thomas's face grew redder by the moment. "He curses us. He swears at us. He is a devil!"

"Please, Brother, charity. Please try to be kind," begged Brother Antonio, squeezing his eyes shut, his face red and splotchy. "Oh, please try to be kind, please."

"No, no, no!" Brother Thomas yelled. "He bit me the last time I tried to bathe him!" Brother Thomas turned his back, folding his arms stubbornly over his chest.

"He spit right in my eyes when I tried to take him to the bathroom. I know how he is," Brother Antonio whispered. "We all have suffered from his abuse."

"No!" Brother Thomas shouted. He would not give an inch. Then, looking at Brother Antonio, he frowned and went on, "It's not so bad being bitten. Or even being spit on. But listen to that!"

Just then, the leprous man began to curse God with such foul words both brothers covered their ears and closed their eyes.

After a moment, Brother Thomas uncovered his ears and opened his eyes. He asked, "If we do nothing and let him go on like that, won't we be as guilty of cursing God as he is? Just by putting up with it and saying nothing?"

Brother Antonio took a long deep breath. Brother Thomas was not the only one who felt that way. All the brothers did. Now no one would take care of the miserable leper.

His bed was foul with urine and feces. His body was caked with perspiration and dirt. The sores from his sickness oozed. Some of his fingers had fallen off. His whole body smelled like rotting flesh. No one dared to try and clean his teeth. They were too afraid he would bite them.

So his mouth smelled like sour milk and rotten eggs. It was even worse when he cursed!

"All of you, go to the devil!" the leper screamed, just as Brother Antonio made up his mind to help the man himself. "The devil eat your livers and the liver of the Mother of God!" the leper roared.

Brother Antonio cringed and covered his ears. How could he say such terrible things?

"He'll have to take care of himself." Brother Thomas said. Turning on a sandaled foot, he almost ran right into Brother Francis, who had just come in the door.

"Ohhhhhhh," Brother Thomas covered his mouth with both hands. "Ohhhhh noooo!"

Brother Antonio dropped his hands to his sides and stared.

"What is all this about?" Brother Francis smiled. Even though his voice was soft and gentle, there was a glint in his dark eyes that drew the truth out of the two brothers.

"Father Francis," Brother Antonio began, his voice suddenly very sad. He called Francis father because Brother Francis was like a father to all of them. "We have been trying to . . . for some time, trying to . . ."

"What is the matter with you idiots?" the leper screamed so loudly Brother Antonio couldn't be heard over the sound of his screams. "Liars! Hypocrites!" The two names were followed by words so horrible even Brother Francis flinched.

"We have been trying to endure this man for some time." Brother Antonio let out a deep sigh of frustration. "He is impossible," he said.

"No matter how kind we are, he curses us. And worse, he curses the Blessed Mother and God!" Brother Thomas said, his voice tearful.

"Even when we try to warn him how harmful his words and actions are to his own soul, he doesn't listen. He seems only to get worse." Brother Antonio hung his head as if it were his fault they could not help the man.

"This man, he is very ill?" Brother Francis asked, looking at each of them.

"Very," they said together.

"You have tried to ease his suffering?"

"And he only grows more hideous every day."

Brother Francis bent his head, his dark eyes misty with tears. Silently, he began to pray.

Brother Antonio and Brother Thomas became very quiet. They, too, bowed their heads.

The prayer of Brother Francis seemed to stretch soothing arms around each of them. Even though the leprous man still yelled his curses, they felt better. Even though the curses beat like fists against their ears, they grew calm. A sense of contentment filled them. Brother Francis was here to help them. The silence that came from the coming of the Holy Spirit, through Brother Francis' prayers, eased their frustration.

"Do not worry," Brother Francis finally said. "I will go to him and care for him myself."

Patting the brothers' arms, Brother Francis went to the cursing man immediately.

The room was dark and smelled of filth. The curtains were closed. But shafts of sunlight revealed the perspiration-stained sheets and covers. The reek of stale sweat and rotting flesh hung like a curtain in the air around the man's bed.

The man turned to them a face covered with sores and twisted with rage and looked at Brother Francis. The expression made the man look strange because he had no nose. It had rotted and fallen off.

But instead of drawing back in horror, Brother Francis greeted him with his arms outstretched. "God give you peace, my dear brother!" he exclaimed.

Cursing loudly the man spit full into Brother Francis' face saying, "What peace can I have from God? He has taken away all my peace. He has taken everything that is good from me!" Throwing a piece of filth at Brother Francis he added, "He has made me rotten and smelly!"

Wiping his face, Brother Francis came to the sick man's bed. Kneeling beside it, as if the odor were roses and violets, Francis smiled. Yet the stench was so strong the leprous man himself almost gagged.

"My dear son, be patient," Brother Francis said, taking one of the man's ravaged hands in his own. "The weaknesses and illnesses of the body are given to us in this world for the salvation of our souls." Because the man grew quiet, he went on, "So if suffering is borne patiently it can be of great merit, of great help to your soul."

"Get away from me, you fool!" the man yelled. "How can I bear patiently all of this pain? Day and night it racks my flesh and bones. Day and night I am tortured, tormented by this horrible sickness!" Tearing patches of hair from his head he screamed filthy words and glared at Brother Francis. "Not only am I suffering from this cursed illness, I have to put up with your imbecile brothers. They torture me. They torment me day and night. They refuse to clean and care for me. None of them serve me the way they should!" Foaming at the mouth the man spit venomously at Brother Francis. "And they call themselves followers of Christ!" With that he beat the bed, blood and filth splattering everywhere.

Tears filled Brother Francis' eyes. He knew the man

was not just troubled with leprosy. His soul was sick, too. He knew this because he had asked the Holy Spirit to help him understand the man's trouble. The man's poor soul was troubled by an evil spirit. That evil spirit made the man discontented, angry and hateful. It even filled the man's mind with filthy words. It encouraged him to say foul things and to curse God and the saints. It encouraged him to refuse to be comforted and contented.

So Brother Francis sadly left the room. Standing alone in the dark hallway, he prayed.

"Dear Jesus," Francis whispered, "you healed many sick and dying with the great wealth of your mercy. You cleansed the cursed ones with the breath of your love; help me to love this poor leper as you do. And help me to ease his soul and his body so that he may come to love you." As Francis prayed, the peace of God's answer filled him up. The cool breath of the Holy Spirit blew into his nostrils, reassuring him.

The whole time Francis stood with eyes closed and hands clasped, the leprous man screamed curses on him and the brothers. He cursed Brother Francis for leaving him and God for giving him the illness.

When he had finished praying, Brother Francis came back into the sick man's room and said, "Dear son, I want to take care of you. Since you are not satisfied with the others, I will help you myself."

The leprous man pressed his sore-encrusted lips together, staring at Brother Francis. Then he answered, "Well, all right. But what more can you do for me than the others?"

Smiling, Brother Francis spread his thin hands and said, "I will do whatever you ask."

That made the man thoughtful. Taking several slow

breaths he considered what Brother Francis had said. Finally he spoke, "Wash me! Wash me all over! I smell so bad, I can't even stand myself!"

"Very well!" Brother Francis said cheerfully. "I will get water and wash you all over!"

Hurrying to the kitchen, Brother Francis boiled water with sweet-smelling herbs in it. When it had cooled enough not to burn the skin he brought it to the leprous man. Undressing him, Brother Francis put all the man's clothes into a bag to be washed. He even changed the bedding. Then he carefully placed the man in a tub and began to wash him with his own hands. Another brother poured the water gently over the man.

As Brother Francis' hands washed the miserable leper's feet the leprosy began to disappear. Then Francis washed his legs. They too were healed! As Francis washed each portion of the leprous man's body, the flesh became new, the sores disappeared!

The water cleansed the man's flesh. Healed by the power of God through Brother Francis' hands, his body became clean. As his body healed, his soul began to heal and be cleansed by the love of God.

"Dear God!" the man exclaimed when he saw his flesh being cured. "Who am I that you would touch me with healing hands?" He began to weep very bitterly, suddenly remembering all the sins he had committed. As he wept more and more, his conscience began to be cleaned through his tears of sorrow for his sins. Slowly the evil and all sin washed away, as if the gentle hand of God held him close to comfort him.

The leprosy healed, and the man's soul was cleansed by his tears of repentance.

"Woe unto me! I deserve to go to the deepest pit of hell

for all the insults and all the curses and hurts I have given to the brothers," he accused himself humbly. Then sobbing loudly into his newly healed hands, he continued, "and for my impatience and blasphemies against God, I deserve the worst torments."

When Brother Francis finished the bath and took away all the soiled sheets and clothing, he came back and comforted the healed leper.

"Such a miracle!" Brother Francis cried, his voice lifting with joy. "God's mercy is so wonderful. It is so vast. It is so deep! He has taken away all your sickness and given you new flesh!" Brother Francis lifted his hands with great joy to the sky. "He has washed away all your sins and made you clean! Thank him, dear brother, thank him!"

The man wept even more, but his tears were tears of joy now. So amazed was he at the mercy of God, he wept for joy and sorrow for his sins for fifteen days! At last, confessing his sins to a priest, he received assurance that God really knew his sorrow and forgave him.

So the miserable leper learned there was mercy in a life of penance and praise, by the divine power of God, through the holy hands of Brother Francis of Assisi.

"It has been

THE Hail & THE Ravenous Wolves

a terrible year," the young man said aloud. "The crops are destroyed from hailstorms." He sniffed and wiped a tear from his cheek. Then, lifting his eyes to the simple crucifix a passing pilgrim had left on a tree, he sighed.

It was a quiet place to pray and not far from the town. The trees provided shade from the sun, protecting whoever knelt by the crucifix. The bushes and shrubs almost made walls to hide the people when they wanted to be alone to pray and worship God.

The young man wanted to be alone. Although it was not an official shrine, the place provided quiet and comfort. It was a place to pray where others could not see him. It made him feel as if he could say anything to the Lord when he was alone. Praying there in the hush of bushes and trees comforted him. But today, he was nervous. A sense of dread hung over him.

"We are not a large town, Lord," he went on, "and our grapes, our corn and our other small crops keep us from starving." Again he wiped away a tear. He was very glad no one could see him crying. He wanted to get up from his knees because the ground was so rocky on the hillside. But instead, he clenched his jaw and stayed, offering his pain for mercy.

"I know we are not the best people," he said softly. "We do things that do not please you. Even people in my own family, who are good Christians, do things that do not please you."

Looking around, he suddenly grew tense. What was

that sound? A bandit sneaking up on him? Or was it just a pilgrim going to the little caves above the wayside shrine? Many of them passed through Greccio, the town he lived in. Then, hearing about the caves, they came up this very path, passing the wayside shrine on their way to the caves.

Listening harder, the young man heard his own breath in his throat. His mouth felt dry. He turned his head, looking from side to side. The cloth of his tunic rustled in his ears. It was terrible to feel such fear. He was young and strong, but terror filled him at knowing he was alone at the wayside shrine. He had never felt afraid here before. Of course, there had never been the terrible disasters as there were now.

"Sorry, Lord," he said, trembling and clutching his rosary in one hand and a large stick in the other. "I thought I heard someone sneaking up on me . . . or something." A long shudder prickled up his back. Lifting his black beads to his lips, he kissed the crucifix. "Lord, I am so afraid," he said. His eyes clouding with tears, he whispered, "The wolves came again this week. This time they attacked two people. Two!" Sniffing loudly, he caught his breath as a bird rustled the bushes nearby.

"Two people, Lord. They attacked two people," the young man continued, "not one alone, but two walking home from the vineyards. And the wolves killed them." Again he shivered before going on. "And last year, Lord, those same ravenous wolves killed sheep and goats and even cattle. Ahhhh!" Weeping softly, he remembered the poor lambs he had lost. "We are poor people, Lord. We are in trouble. We need your help."

In a small cave not far up the hill, Brother Francis had been praying. But the sadness and desperation in the young man's voice carried on the breeze and whispered in the solitude of his hermitage. Ravenous wolves? And hailstorms? Brother Francis lifted his bearded chin and turned his gaunt face toward the sound of the voice.

"It is true, Lord, things go on. People do bad things." The young man's voice was choked with sorrow. "But who can tell them to stop? Ah Lord, no one would listen to me." He sighed softly and began to pray his rosary aloud.

The Hail Marys rolled quietly over the quivering sound of the breeze passing through the bushes. Brother Francis' heart melted. "Oh, what a pitiful thing," Francis cried to the Lord, "that these people should suffer such disasters!"

Getting to his feet, Francis walked down the rocky path to the little shrine. The young man had just finished his prayers and looked up very startled when Brother Francis came out of the bushes.

"You frightened me!" the young man gasped, scrambling to his feet. "I thought you were a bandit or . . ."

"The ravenous wolves?" Brother Francis asked, trying to smile reassuringly. "God hears your prayers, little brother."

"He does?"

"Yes, he truly does," Brother Francis said, motioning the young man to come with him.

"How I hope he does," the young man sighed and looked at the pilgrim out of the corner of his eyes. He had seen many beggars and even more pilgrims, but there was something different about this man. The way he smiled seemed to make the path brighter. His patched robe and his worn sandals were like those of other pilgrims, yet the bright hope shining from this one's dark eyes seemed to surround him and calm him. When he walked beside this pilgrim, the shadows reaching out from the tall trees seemed harmless. They no longer made him feel the terrible dread. It was as if this pilgrim carried a lamp inside him and it shone out of the inky depths like moonlight shone on dark water, making everything plain.

Brother Francis walked beside the young man, looking across the valley at the destruction the hailstorms had caused. The corn was withered and crushed to the ground. The grapevines blackened and damaged by the cold and their battered leaves looked pitiful. Not much was left to produce a harvest.

"There will be poor crops again. Many of us will go hungry," the young man said, noticing the pilgrim looking at the fields. "Besides this devastation," he went on in a timid voice, "there are the wolves."

"Wolves," Brother Francis shook his head, his thin face very sad. "Wolves taking the lives of men, women and children. How terrible."

The young man stared at him in wonder. This pilgrim was not frightened! Why? A pilgrim alone in the mountains, alone on his holy journey would be easy prey for such hungry wolves.

"They have killed many people, and a great number of livestock," the young man said, awe in his voice.

"It is a terrible thing to offend the Living God," Brother Francis answered gently, "for it is he who allows these tribulations to come upon us. He allows it so we will turn to him, repent and ask for mercy."

Nodding, the youth agreed quickly. The words frightened him. But the gentleness of Brother Francis' compassion made the youth want to stay and listen to Francis. "You must come and speak to my family," the young man said, feeling a new hope inside.

"I will," Brother Francis agreed easily. "I will go to the

town's well. There I will speak to all who gather there and listen."

So the young man hurried home to fetch bread for the compassionate pilgrim and to tell his family. Excitement stirred in his heart. He told his father what had happened. He told his mother. He told their neighbor to the east and their neighbor to the south.

Those neighbors told their neighbors. And those neighbors told theirs, until all the town gathered by the well to hear the compassionate pilgrim.

The little brother, as Brother Francis called the young man, hurried to the well, carrying a loaf of bread and a small piece of goat cheese wrapped in a cloth. He pushed through all the people.

'How astonishing that so many have already come in such a short time!' he thought.

Brother Francis' small form was almost lost in the great number of people. Above them, the clouds rolling and tumbling in the dusky blue sky turned slate gray. A wind rose and a chill bit through the people's clothes. They shivered and wailed in fear.

"Not more hail!" a woman cried. A frightened whisper passed from person to person. As the crowd grew more and more terrified the sound of a wolf's howl split the quiet, followed by a crack of thunder!

"Brothers, sisters," Brother Francis lifted his hands high into the air. His patched robe swirled around his thin body. "Listen to me! God has heard the voices of those who are praying for help . . ."

"The hail is coming!" someone bleated, the voice caught in the roar of the wind and carried away like a leaf.

"No! The hail will not come! The ravenous wolves will not come!" Turning, Francis opened his arms as if he would embrace them all. "Hear me!" As he raised his voice the wind died to a soft whisper. "To honor God Almighty and to give glory to his holy name, I promise you all these terrible things will stop!" Brother Francis' voice rose above the fearful cries of the people.

The wind had stopped. Only the sounds of children whimpering and the muffled tears of people who held their faces in their hands broke the quiet.

Slowly, the people began to look at Francis, their faces puzzled and then full of astonishment, their eyes wide. Their mouths fell open. Some began to pray as fear prickled up their backs and over their arms.

"How is it the wind and the thunder obey him?" many whispered.

"God will shower his blessings on you if you trust me." Brother Francis' voice sounded loud in the wake of the whispers. Then, as if God, too, listened to the little poor man's words and wanted the people to hear him, a stream of light broke through the darkened clouds pouring down on Brother Francis.

"What should we do?" A man's gruff voice broke the hushed silence. "Tell us!"

"Do you want mercy?" Brother Francis asked, raising his hands to the heavens again.

"Yes!" someone shouted.

"Yes! Yes!" Voices swelled in the quiet air.

"Then you must confess your sins." Brother Francis' dark eyes shone with a fierce light as if he saw all the cruel and ugly things that had been done by the people. "You know what things offend God. Those of you who have told lies, stolen, cheated, gossiped, listened to gossip and hated—these sins burn in your souls. You cannot hide them from the Lord. Even if you hide them in the most secret place in your hearts, the Lord sees!"

Many faces burned red with guilt. Chins dropped with shame.

"Do you think by pretending to be innocent of sin that your sins will go away and that God will forgive you?" Pausing only for a moment, Francis went on, his eyes like glowing embers, "Only sorrow for offending God and turning away from sinning again will bring forgiveness."

Though many listened and heard, there were some faces that turned away.

"When your neighbor offends you, do you forgive him if he does not show sorrow? No! Do you forgive him if he pretends he did not hurt, cheat or offend you? No!" Pausing, Francis drew a long careful breath, tears running down his face. "You forgive him when he confesses, admits he has offended you and asks to be forgiven and promises not to hurt you again." Brother Francis' voice grew soft but fervent. "Go and make good confessions. Start doing what is good and right. Be kind. Love one another. Do good and bring God's gladness and mercy into your lives."

The sounds of weeping began and grew louder and louder, all the people looking at their own hearts and seeing how their wrongdoing offended God. Brother Francis' lips moved in prayer. His face was alight with fervor. His body trembled as more and more souls repented, going down on their knees. Yet, he saw those whose hearts were still hardened. They did not want to confess their sins. They did not want to look into their own hearts. Some even started to walk away!

"I promise you this, too!" Brother Francis called after them, his voice suddenly deep and very loud like thunder. It carried to every ear. "If you are ungrateful and go back to your old ways, the wolves will come back. The hailstorms will pour down on you, and all your afflictions will be worse than ever. You will starve, suffer and become prey to the ravenous wolves. Life will be a living hell, for you will provoke the anger of God. You will reap his justice for refusing to repent and turn away from evil." Brother Francis' voice shook, tears flooding down his gaunt cheeks.

Francis' words, the very sight of him, drove the rest of the people to their knees. There was a great turning away from the evil ways in Greccio that day. And the little Brother Francis moved on.

From then on, all the townspeople repented, confessed and began to change their ways. The danger passed. The wolves seemed to disappear and come no more. The hailstorms stopped. The crops grew full, bursting with life and fruit. Though storms did harm other areas near Greccio, the little town remained untouched. When a storm threatened, the young man whose prayers Brother Francis had heard watched it come. As it drew close it would either stop or change its course. But then it would leave the area and the town would remain unhurt.

"The hail and the wolves keep their pact," the young man would say, "as long as we obey the laws of our good God." And he would remember the compassion shining in the dark eyes of the pilgrim, Brother Francis of Assisi. The memory of it gave him hope, hope in God's mercy.

"What a beautiful day,"

Brother Masseo's Wild WHiRLiNG

Brother Masseo grinned at Brother Francis, his wide face full of joy. Sauntering next to the smaller man his happiness was contagious. "Birds are singing. The air is cool and crisp. There is the smell of wood smoke and herbs on the breeze!" Brother Masseo closed his eyes, reveling in his enjoyment. It was a fine day to go about preaching the Word of God.

"Truly a wonderful day," Brother Francis agreed.

"Look at the road, Brother!" Brother Masseo waved a large hand at the road. It unfolded in twists and turns ahead. He could see people moving all along its length. "I see pilgrims, merchants, people going to market." Grinning again, he went on, "Truly all of us are finding it a perfect day to travel." All he needed was a nod and smile from Brother Francis to feel even more full of happiness.

Brother Masseo's joy was especially strong because he felt special. Often Brother Francis asked him to go with him on his journeys, and that, Brother Masseo felt, was a very special privilege.

Walking slightly ahead, Brother Masseo sang softly. The tune was about the goodness of God's creation, one of Brother Francis' favorites. Brother Masseo felt like swelling up and popping with happiness. People noticed him. He could see them looking at him from the corners of their eyes, or taking quick, or even long looks as they passed. They were noticing him because he was with Brother Francis. He couldn't help feeling a little like they were noticing how poor and, Brother Masseo chuckled to himself, how humble they were.

'We are so poor,' Brother Masseo thought, with a sideways glance at a merchant leading a donkey piled high with his merchandise, 'we are so poor we don't even own cloaks to keep us warm.'

Grinning, Brother Masseo pondered the thought as they walked. Being poor gave him a feeling of being free, of having nothing to lose. He liked that feeling. He liked feeling different from everyone else. As they came to a crossroad where three roads met, he paused, turning to Brother Francis.

Travellers went steadily around them. Some nodded their hellos, while others passed, too absorbed in their own thoughts to notice them.

"So, Brother Francis," Brother Masseo smiled, "which way shall we go?"

Brother Francis returned the smile, and closing his eyes he took a long deep breath, standing perfectly still.

Patiently, Brother Masseo waited, his smile somewhat smaller as Brother Francis inhaled as if he tasted the air. But Francis showed no signs of answering. Just as Brother Masseo was about to speak, Brother Francis answered, "We shall take the road God wants us to take." He spoke cheerfully, his dark eyes popped open, his thin mouth curved in a smile.

"And how will we know which road God wants us to take?" Brother Masseo asked, laughing softly.

Brother Francis suddenly became very serious, his thin face lined with purpose. "By the sign I will show you," he said.

Brother Masseo nodded, becoming a little uncomfortable as people began to stare at the two poor pilgrims standing in the middle of the crossroads talking.

"Okay," Brother Masseo cleared his throat, hoping Brother Francis would not take too long to decide. "One goes to Siena, one goes to Florence and one goes to Arezzo. Which shall we take?"

"Now," Brother Francis began, raising his dark brows, "under the merit of holy obedience, I command you to whirl around and around and around at this crossroad!"

"Here?" Brother Masseo's mouth fell open. He could still feel people watching. Surely Brother Francis could not be serious!

"Right where you are standing, just as children do. And do not stop turning until I tell you!"

"Okay." Brother Masseo did not even consider going against Brother Francis' command, even though he was embarrassed. But as he began to whirl, he began to feel more and more foolish.

He whirled round and round and round, until the whole world seemed to be spinning! He whirled around so long that he tumbled to the ground.

"Get up!" Brother Francis cried, urging Brother Masseo to continue.

Stumbling to his feet, Brother Masseo whirled some more! He fell again and again was urged to his feet.

Laughter washed over him. Jeers and shouts bombarded him. Some of the people passing even called him "mad." But he kept whirling.

Finally Brother Francis yelled, "Stand still! Don't move!"

And Brother Masseo stood still, swaying and tilting, trying to keep his balance. But the world would not stop spinning.

"What direction are you facing?" Brother Francis

asked, excitement in his voice.

Brother Masseo squinted his eyes and clenched his teeth until the world stopped swaying. "Toward Siena," he said, his face red with embarrassment.

"Then that is the road God wants us to take!" Brother Francis said, utterly serious.

At once they began to walk down the road toward Siena. Brother Masseo marveled that Brother Francis did not seem to notice the grins and comments of the people on the same road.

'Why?' Brother Masseo thought. 'Why did he make me whirl in such a childish way?' Sneaking a look at his companion, he shook his head. Brother Francis was smiling. The look of contentment did not tell Brother Masseo what the little brother was thinking. It did not tell him if Brother Francis realized the embarrassment he had caused Brother Masseo.

Cheeks still burning, Brother Masseo could not hide his feelings. 'What foolishness,' he thought. 'As if God would choose such a crazy way to reveal his will.' His respect for Brother Francis kept him from revealing what he was thinking, but he could not help wondering if the other man wasn't a little "mad" like people whispered behind his back.

After some time they drew closer to Siena. Brother Masseo was very serious now. His joy in the journey had evaporated under humiliation. Much to his surprise, some of the citizens of Siena recognized Brother Francis and rushed to greet him.

"Brother Francis, what a great honor it is to see you!" one wealthy merchant said, almost lifting the little man off his feet with a hug.

"Good tidings, welcome back!" another called.

"Our house is yours!" still another said. And before Brother Masseo knew it, they were nearly swept off their feet and escorted into the city. "We are so glad you have come!" the people cried.

Brother Masseo grinned, his happiness beginning to return. But his smile vanished as the crowd scattered. The people left them standing near a small group of men fighting with swords. Keeping a distance, they whispered in fear and horror.

"What is this?" Brother Francis gasped, his voice breaking with sorrow. Rushing to the side of two men lying in a great pool of blood, he lifted first one of their heads and then the other. They were both dead.

Brother Masseo hurried to Brother Francis, helping him back to his feet. The look of grief on his companion's face brought tears to his own eyes. But fear made his stomach turn over as the men continued to fight, ignoring the two brothers.

The clashing of swords and angry curses echoed off the stone buildings. The shuffle of fast-moving feet and the whirl of cloth in hot air made the fighting even more real, even more frightening.

"Stop!" Brother Francis cried, pulling free of Brother Masseo's hands. "Stop, good brothers. Stop!" Stepping suddenly between two swords, Brother Francis did not even flinch as the shining blades lunged at his stomach. But both men were quick enough to turn aside.

"Are you crazy?" one of them yelled, his face dark with rage. There was a long, bleeding slash down his cheek. Blood stained his fine tunic and breeches. His eyes squinted in anger as he panted for breath.

"Stop, please," Brother Francis' gentleness was like a hand persistently tugging on the bridle of a horse. "It is

God's good pleasure to give life, sir." Brother Francis' voice, barely a whisper, turned the fighting men's heads. "It is God's good pleasure to take life."

"And mine, if the rogues get in my way," one of the men growled. His sword trembled in his hand.

"Would you kill a fellow man, trading the hope of heaven for the curse of hell?"

For a moment, there was only the shuffling of feet and the muttering of protests.

"Life is too precious to end it because of a quarrel," Brother Francis said softly. "Look at you," Francis went on before any could interrupt, spreading his hands pleadingly. "Each of you is a special creation of our wonderful Lord's. Each of you is cleansed with the beauty and power of baptism." Turning to each of the men who were holding swords, he raised his brows and asked, "Will you spill blood upon the snowy carpet of your souls? Will you cut into the flesh of God's own Son?"

Brother Masseo flinched. Some of the people in the crowd gasped.

"For every stroke you strike upon the flesh of your fellow man falls upon the holy body of our risen Lord. And with each wound we give him more anguish than the small pain we suffer by being wronged by our fellow men." Brother Francis turned, tears streaking his dark cheeks. "Strike me instead!" he said, "I beg you! For I cannot bear to see you wound my Lord!" Taking the blade of the nearest sword he placed it upon his own neck.

The man pulled gently away, shame replacing his anger, tears in his eyes. Slowly the men put their swords and knives away, unable to lift their eyes to Brother Francis' anguished face.

"We are all brothers!" Brother Francis said raising his

voice. "Let us live together as brothers. Let us give our harmony back to the great God who gives us life, harmony as an offering of thanksgiving! How small is that gift for the precious life still swelling in our breasts!"

Bringing two of the men's hands together, Brother Francis sealed the beautiful peace. His eyes bright with affection, he nodded at the others until they all clasped hands.

Brother Masseo bowed his head, his eyes brimming with tears. 'What wonder this is,' he thought, 'that we should come to Siena and find a feud of blood. What a wonder this is.' Brother Masseo was looking at the now smiling countenance of Brother Francis. 'To think that I should be the instrument of God's will, that he should use the foolish whirling of a prideful brother to bring a holy man to soothe and save souls. What a marvelous thing it is that God will use the foolish ways of men to demonstrate his wisdom.'

As Brother Masseo thought these things, he finally saw the hand of God in his wild whirling. When he looked at Brother Francis, he was surprised to find him looking back at him.

"Amen," Brother Francis said. And Brother Masseo was certain Brother Francis knew the thoughts of his very heart.

"Peace I give to thee. My peace, note, not as the world gives it do I give it to thee," Brother Francis said, reminding Brother Masseo of Jesus' promise in the holy Word of God. "Peace and goodness," he whispered in the ear of his greatly humbled companion Brother Masseo.

This story recalls James 1:2, 3, 12;
James 5:7, 11; Luke 8:4–15 and Luke
21:19.

"He's coming!

THE Multiplication **of the** Grapes

He's coming!" The man rushed up the road leading from Rieti toward the little church two miles from town. Huffing and puffing, he moved quickly for a man his size. His brow running with perspiration, he squinted his hazel eyes. "He's going to stay at the church!" he told the small group of people sitting by the side of the road.

"Oh, here?" asked a thin man with a drooping moustache. "Why would he stay here? There is no butcher, no market, no place to get food?"

"He is already here!" said another man, who was carrying a cloth sack tied to a stick.

"What do you mean he is here?" the first man panted. "He was supposed to go to Rieti. A friend of mine heard the news from two merchants."

"Why are you so impatient, Stephano?" sighed the man with the moustache. "We will all hear him. Why do you think we have come?"

"I want to hear what he has to say now!" Stephano puffed out his chest and round belly. Suddenly he looked very important. "Time, I have no time. My wife will soon have a baby. My mother's birthday is almost upon us. And soon the grapes will be ready to pick and press." Stephano was still panting. He stopped, suddenly realizing he was no longer out of breath.

"Why did you come if you do not have time to listen?"

The thin man twisted the ends of his moustache. Dropping his voice to a whisper, he said, "I have heard this Brother Francis' words bring miracles."

"Miracles! Nonsense!" Stephano sputtered. "I am here because my wife will give me no peace until I satisfy her curiosity." Looking around, he, too, dropped his voice, "If it was not for the baby I think she would have dropped everything and come herself!"

"Oh no!"

"Ah, you poor man."

"Really? She has such a mind of her own?" The small group of listeners shook their heads in amazement.

"Get it over with, I say," Stephano sputtered loudly. "Life is hard enough without being driven by your wife."

"Or your husband," said a woman in the crowd ahead of them.

"You left in such a hurry, what did you bring to eat?" the man with the moustache asked Stephano, changing the subject.

"Eat?" Stephano threw his hands up. "I don't intend to be here very long. Besides," he grunted, looking around at the vineyard, "I can always eat grapes." Picking a few bunches, he stuffed his mouth as the group began to move toward the church. There were more and more people as they got closer.

"Slow down, Stephano," the thin man said, shaking his head. "You are always in such a hurry to arrive, you never enjoy the journey."

"What journey? One leg goes after the other," Stephano said through a mouthful of grapes, almost choking.

"You are going to choke to death," Bennini said, pulling on his moustache nervously.

"No time to slow down and enjoy a journey, Bennini.

Too much to do." Stephano cleared his throat. "I barely have time to do my morning prayers. If God hears, it is because he can make out the words without pauses between them."

A few people chuckled, nodding in agreement. Bennini frowned.

"Look," The moustached Bennini said, pointing to the church.

The little brother everyone called Francis and another brother came out of the church.

"May the Lord bless you," Brother Francis spoke while standing a distance from them, his companion standing close by, his hand under Brother Francis' arm. He seemed to be supporting him.

"Look how thin he is," Stephano whispered, picking another bunch of grapes.

"He probably does not take time to eat," someone joked softly.

"Ha ha!" Stephano laughed. "Let him eat grapes like the rest of us who hurried here to hear him."

"Patience, my dear brothers and sisters. I know you have come a long way and I thank you for your deep desire to hear the word of God. Settle down and be patient." It was almost as if the little brother was speaking directly to Stephano. "Patience is an act of kindness. Be patient in waiting for that which you desire. Be patient with one another. Our Father in heaven has great patience with us." Looking up into the sky Brother Francis opened his dark eyes wide.

"Look how his eyes shine!" Bennini whispered.

"Shhh," someone hushed him as the crowd of people pressed forward, stirring at the words of Brother Francis.

"Try to wait patiently. Behold!" Brother Francis

smiled, opening his arms wide. "Look how patiently the grower of these grapes must wait for the rains to come and nourish the vines. So we, too, must endure one another waiting for our needs." Turning, Francis looked from face to face. "Do we not think those who endure hardship are blessed? You have heard of the patience of Job and seen how his patience bore the fruit of mercy and compassion from God."

Stephano listened to the murmur of voices agreeing with the little brother. Though he knew Brother Francis was speaking to all of them, it was as if a pin were pricking his heart, as if the little man spoke directly to him.

"Are you tempted to run from one work to another without praying for God's help and blessing? Are you tempted to hurry past the church and to avoid making a sign of love, such as the Sign of the Cross, because you are too busy? Or maybe you hear Mass quickly, or mutter your prayers in half-taken breaths? 'Time,' you say, 'I have no time!'" Brother Francis' eyes ran with tears. "My brethren, count it as joy when you have these temptations!"

Breaking off, Francis seemed to steady himself and take a deep breath. "You see," he continued, lowering his voice as if to tell a secret, "when your faith is tested, God strengthens you in patience!"

"So, I am without strength now," Stephano complained softly, but his words were without conviction.

"Blessed is the man who endures temptation, and endures patiently! For when he comes to the very end of those temptations and he has not given in, God will give him a crown of life!" Brother Francis' voice rose, a stirring clear sound that carried to every ear. "And all those who love him shall receive this treasure."

Stephano sank down next to his friend Bennini.

Together they watched the little brother go back into the church. More people arrived. Stephano heard many of them speaking excitedly about hearing Brother Francis. Some waited impatiently, as he had.

"He spoke for such a short time," Bennini said slowly, offering a piece of bread to Stephano from his bag. They both picked more grapes and continued to eat. The grapes tasted very refreshing in the heat.

"He will come out again," Stephano said, taking the bread. He felt Bennini looking at him. He was amazed at the new sound in his own voice. It was as if the words of the brother had already begun to take root. He, Stephano, spoke patiently.

Inside the church was cool and quiet. The odors of wax and incense filled the room. Brother Francis rested, a cool cloth laid across his eyes.

"I don't know why we must stay here so long," Brother Tobias said softly. "Your eyes are hurting and we must get to Rieti because the cardinal may have medicines to help."

"In time," Brother Francis' mouth twitched in a gentle smile. "There are so many people who know I am coming, so many who hunger after the Word of God. We must stay a little while. We must speak to those we can, and then we will go to Rieti, by a back way, perhaps."

"Were you speaking to me, Brother Francis?" Brother Tobias asked in a small voice. "I mean, about patience?"

Brother Francis' hearty laugh surprised him.

"Oh, little Brother," he laughed, "I was speaking about myself!"

Brother Tobias laughed quietly with him. And though he said nothing, he could hardly believe that Brother Francis felt impatience.

"Excuse me, Brothers." The pastor of the church

stopped a little distance away, his face lined with worry. "Is there anything I can get you?" he asked.

Though the pastor spoke quietly, something in his voice made Brother Francis uncover his eyes. At least, so Brother Tobias thought. But in reality, Brother Francis could see into the priest's good heart and knew what was troubling him.

"Are there more pilgrims outside?" Brother Francis asked gently.

"Many more," the priest sighed. But still he would not say what it was that bothered him.

"We are fine, Father," Brother Tobias started to say, hoping to continue talking to Brother Francis alone.

"Yes, we are." Brother Francis spoke as he rose carefully to his feet. Crossing to the priest, Francis took his hands. "My dear Father," he said kindly, "how many measures of grapes does your little vineyard produce each year?" Then, cocking his dark head, he added with a smile, "When it produces well, that is?"

The priest's cheeks flushed, but he did not pull his hands away. "Twelve measures, little Brother."

"Twelve," lifting his black brows, Brother Francis nodded. There was a long pause. Francis' eyes filled with the light of prayer. Then he said, "I beg you, Father, to bear patiently with my staying here in your church. Please," inhaling a deep breath of the cool air in the little church, Brother Francis continued, "I have been terribly ill and the quiet, the rest I find in this holy place is doing me good."

The worry melted from the priest's eyes, but before he could agree, Brother Francis held up a thin hand.

"Let the pilgrims take as many grapes as they need to quench their thirst and relieve their hunger. Do this for the love of God, and maybe even for my poor little self's sake."

"I want to let them," the priest said slowly, "I love the Lord, but the vineyard, little Brother, supports the church, my needs and many of the poor. If the pilgrims eat all the grapes . . ."

"I promise you, on behalf of my Lord Jesus Christ," Brother Francis said, lifting his hands toward the crucifix over the altar, "I promise you that this year, you will get twenty measures of grapes from your vines."

The priest's eyes grew very wide. He opened his mouth to protest, as he knew how quickly the grapes were being eaten. But he did not speak. His throat grew dry. His heart beat against his ribs. What was he feeling? His eyes turned to the crucifix. Hope? Excitement? Foolishness?

"Oh, Father!" Brother Francis said, suddenly carried away by a surge of joy. "Did you see their faces when I spoke of the Lord's promises? Did you see how many of them had tears in their eyes at the special promise of life? The Lord is working a great wonder here if we will just be patient." With a hopeful little smile, Francis turned eyes filled with a supernatural fire to the face of the priest.

"Let us not stop the hand of the Lord," the priest agreed heartily. After making certain the brothers were comfortable, he went back to his duties.

So Brother Francis went out to speak again and again. The last time so many people were present the vines were nearly naked.

"You have heard the parable of the Sower of Seed. How first, the seed sown falls by the wayside and the devil takes it away. How second, it falls upon the rock and has no roots and so temptation takes it away. And how last, it falls among the thorns and is choked out by the pleasures and cares of this life. That seed, my friends, is the Word of God." Brother Francis' voice was strong and firm. "Finally, how the Word comes to those of good heart and they hear the Word of God." Brother Francis' excitement sent a ripple of whispering through the crowd. "And when they hear, they bring forth good fruit, in patience."

Pausing, Francis drew a long breath, then opened his arms wide and, smiling, went on, saying, "Patience, dear Brethren. Good fruit comes from the soul through patience. Let us not rush through our lives. Let us not hurry. Let us perform each work carefully, as if we were doing every act and thinking every thought for God's good. Let us pray slowly, with meaning in our words. Let us listen to the Word of God attentively, so it will take root in our hearts and become a part of our lives."

Lifting up his eyes to the hopeful faces, Francis said, "For in your practice of patience you shall possess your souls. Through patiently living your lives for God, you will not lose your souls. Patience is a powerful path, a path where compassion replaces cruelty, where mercy outlives intolerence. It is through being patient that we learn to walk in the will of God. When we go slowly, we hear him. We discover his mercy and goodness in our lives. And, at last, through patience comes his peace, that beautiful quietness of heart and soul that fills you up and will not leave room for worry. When you do not worry you see more clearly. When you walk you cannot trip and fall. When you go slowly and prayerfully you will not fall. You will be upheld by the strength of his continued presence in your life and soul, just by taking time to see him. In patience, dear people, you shall possess your souls."

Once again the people grew quiet. The soft rustle of cloth and the gentle footfalls of those moving away followed the pause, as Brother Francis lowered his eyes and went back into the church.

The priest nodded to himself, watching the people and marveling at the changes he saw in many of their eyes. 'In your patience you shall possess your souls. I must be patient,' he thought, as the vision of his grapes being stripped from the vines and disappearing into the people's mouths came back to him.

Brother Francis stayed for many days. By the time the people began to leave, there were only a few pitiful bunches of grapes left on the vines.

After the people were gone, the priest went out to pick the grapes that were left on the vines. Staring at the small handful, he shook his head sadly. Putting them in the basket, he turned to go. As he glanced down he saw another bunch. 'Must have missed this one,' he thought, putting it into the basket, too. With a sigh, he started to walk away, and he saw another bunch! He picked it. There was another and another and another. Filling basket after basket the priest moved through the devastated vineyard almost stunned. Twelve measures of grapes, thirteen . . . He kept picking. There were more and more!

Fifteen, seventeen! "How is this possible?" he gasped. "Twenty measures!" the priest cried out, his eyes full of amazement. "Blessed be the name of the Lord."

From the stripped and nearly devastated vines the priest filled his baskets with twenty measures of grapes to make wine. It was just as little Brother Francis promised.

Starting home, Stephano heard about the miracle. He nodded his large head and made the Sign of the Cross. Then, slapping Bennini on the back, he laughed louder than he had in many years. "The little brother brought miracles after all," he said.

"Well," Bennini laughed, twirling his moustache. "He brought the miracles and you finally got to hear him and satisfy your wife's curiosity. So let us hurry home so you can tell her and get her off your back."

"Patience, Bennini," Stephano wagged a finger at him, taking a great breath of air. "I refuse to lose my soul over an impatient wife. No," he licked his lips, his nostrils flared, "there is something to the little brother's words about patience. Something, that is . . ." He struggled to think of a word to describe what he had heard.

"Something fruitful?" Bennini suggested, his eyebrows up.

"Ah, yes. Like the multiplication of the grapes, Bennini. The word of God is fruit in my soul. I just have to listen."

"Me, too, my friend," Bennini smiled, feeling cheerful. "What will you tell your good wife when she asks what the brother spoke about?"

Stephano lengthened his stride. Then stretching, as the sun hovered on the horizon, he said, "I will tell her 'Be patient, woman, you will hear in God's good time!'"

So it was that the little Brother Francis of Assisi's good words brought a multiplication of virtues in the people at the small vineyard. And that happened by the same hand of God that multiplied the grapes for the love of Jesus and for the sake of his little poor man of Assisi.

Something

was troubling Brother Francis. Brother Leo could tell. There was a quietness about him, a sadness that disturbed Brother Leo. Francis' eyes seemed moist with unshed tears of sorrow when they were usually filled with joy.

THE Virtue of Fear

In spite of the sadness, it was a splendid day. The sun shone brightly, with not a cloud marring the clear blue sky. The shining white ball of the sun quickly began to warm the earth. Dew glistened and a gentle breeze brought the smell of newly cut grass and damp earth to the two brothers walking side by side down the road.

Inhaling long and slowly, Brother Leo could not help smiling. "Please, God, may we have many days as perfect as this one," Brother Leo said, hoping to cheer up Brother Francis.

Brother Francis tipped his head up and sucked in a long breath. "Ah," he said, "how fresh the morning air is. You are right!"

Brother Leo sighed. "You know, Brother Francis, a great many young men have joined us lately," he grinned, "and that is a joy."

"Yes," said Brother Francis, nodding and scratching his dark beard and knitting his brow. "So many come, by God's grace."

"And only a few leave," Brother Leo said, trying to stay cheerful. But Brother Leo's mind wandered to a certain brother who had appeared so holy and contented, and yet, he had not stayed. He had left Brother Francis' little Way and gone back to the worldly ways. Brother Leo knew this was what was troubling Brother Francis.

Brother Leo peeked out of the corner of his eye at Brother Francis. "I wonder," he mused out loud, "why he left." Hoping that talking about it would help Brother Francis feel better, he waited.

Without glancing over, Brother Francis said, "Look, Brother Leo, do you see that farmer?"

Far across the newly cut field a farmer worked, bending, rising, bending, rising. He seemed to be gathering bundles of grass.

"Such slow, hot work," Brother Leo said, feeling sorry for the farmer.

"But look how hard he works!" Brother Francis cried, his face a mask of appreciation. Turning to Brother Leo, he said, "Do you think he has the virtue of perseverance?"

Brother Leo's eyebrows shot up. "Of course. He isn't giving up!"

"But why isn't he? It is such terribly hard work." Brother Francis asked rather more to himself than Brother Leo.

They continued walking in silence. Up the road came a tattered looking man pulling a wagon full of chickens in crates.

"Look at this poor man," Brother Leo whispered, "he doesn't even have enough to buy a horse or a donkey to pull his cart." Shaking his head, he grew very quiet. Then he added, "Even his clothes are tattered and patched. He is almost a beggar."

As the man passed, he paused, raising his beat-up hat and smiled. "Good morning, Brothers," he said in a low cheerful voice.

"Good morning, and the peace of the Lord be upon you!"

Brother Francis bent his head, almost bowing to the peasant.

When the man had passed by, Brother Francis asked Brother Leo, "Do you think he had the virtue of poverty?"

"Well!" Brother Leo glanced back over his shoulder. "He certainly appeared to be poor. And the contentment in his eyes, even his smile would lead you to believe he accepted the simplicity of his life as a gift, or rather as the will of God."

Brother Francis stopped in the shade of a large olive tree. Wiping perspiration from his brow, he asked, "Why doesn't he give up such a hard life? Because God has given it to him? Poverty, such a beautiful virtue."

Brother Leo glanced over. Many people did not think so much of poverty. They did not understand that the little poor man was trying to help them to see that poverty of spirit was not being overly attached to the things of the world, and it was loving God more than the things and people of the world. That was the poverty Francis loved so dearly, the poverty that he expressed by refusing to own any possessions.

So Brother Leo did not comment. He really wasn't sure Brother Francis was talking to him.

Once again they continued their journey, but now Brother Francis spoke softly, as if to himself. Brother Leo did not interrupt. He had heard Francis speak this way many times when he was trying to sort out a problem.

"So," Brother Francis said, lifting his chin and studying the cloudless sky, "there are many virtues. There is humility. A wonderful virtue, one that protects the heart from being misled by self-love."

Brother Leo nodded, even though he knew Brother Francis was speaking aloud to consider different ideas.

"Humility, humility, humility. It is a most wondrous virtue that teaches the heart to see the beauty of God." Here Francis paused and said, "Did he know this virtue?" Nodding slowly, he continued, "I really think he did know it. Don't you?"

Brother Leo looked over to see if the little brother expected an answer. But Brother Francis was speaking to the far off hills, shining green in the distance. "Yes, that certain brother knew it," he said finally.

"What about patience?" Brother Francis asked suddenly. "Patience, patience, patience. I remember many times when his patience was tried through terrible tribulation, like fire! Yes," he said, "that dear special brother who left us had patience."

Brother Leo swallowed. He could see tears in Brother Francis' eyes. He was sorry he had brought up the subject. Brother Francis had been so fond of the brother who left that talking about it had made him even sadder.

"Abstinence," Brother Francis went on. "Now that is a tough virtue."

"Yes it is!" Brother Leo said, trying to sound cheerful.

"Did he have it?" Turning, Francis cocked a brow at Brother Leo as he said, "I think so. Yes, I think he did."

Brother Leo looked away.

"Poverty, perseverance, charity, patience, chastity, hope, faith . . . so many," Brother Francis' voice dropped to a trembling whisper, "Did he know all of these?"

Biting his lip, Brother Leo frowned. Poor Brother Francis. It was impossible not to see the pain in his dark eyes. He was trying so hard to understand why the brother left.

'What can I say?' Brother Leo thought. 'People leave for all kinds of reasons. And most of the time they do not tell you why.' Leo forced himself to look at Brother Francis and said, "What other virtue is there?"

"Fear!" Brother Francis said, suddenly straightening, his hands opened wide. He lifted them as if he were offering the answer to the puzzle to heaven. "Fear, fear, fear, dear Brother, it was fear!"

Licking his lips, Brother Leo looked puzzled. "Fear," he repeated.

"Not fear as in terror!" Brother Francis said excitedly. "Fear of God, fear of offending the great goodness of God! Do you know this virtue?" Brother Francis' voice boomed with fervor, startling Brother Leo. "Yes," Brother Francis said, answering himself, "you do, dear Brother Leo. But, alas." Brother Francis looked into Brother Leo's eyes and took him by both shoulders. "Alas, that poor brother fell and left our brotherhood because he had no fear."

The look of sadness was so powerful in Brother Francis' eyes tears came to Brother Leo's.

Glancing back, Brother Francis pointed to the farmer still working in the hot field. "The farmer does not give up because he fears God."

Brother Leo stared at the tiny figure so far away.

"He understands that to go against God's purpose for him would cause more grief," Francis continued. "And any pleasure he could find would be useless against such grief. Fear, dear Brother, fear of God."

"And the peasant pulling the cart?" Brother Leo asked, remembering the tattered man.

"He, too, had the virtue of fear," Brother Francis gulped a quick breath, excited by the light of understanding God had put into his mind. "The peasant's contentment revealed his possession of fear of God."

"Ah, I see," Brother Leo nodded. "He loved God and so,

in his love, he did not want to offend him."

"Yes, he feared to offend him. For by going against God he would bring unhappiness on himself," Brother Francis said. "Fear of God is respecting God, and knowing that doing his will brings blessings. But going against his will brings punishment and tribulations." Brother Francis stopped at the bridge crossing a stream. He said, "I understand now. I shall pray for our departed brother that he will acquire the virtue of fear of God."

"I shall, also," Brother Leo said with a sigh of relief. He was so glad to see the sadness gone from his dear friend.

"Come, dear Brother, let us go down and quench our thirst at the river."

"Only if it is God's will," Brother Leo grinned.

Suddenly, Brother Francis threw his head back and laughed. Then, slapping Brother Leo on the back, he said, "How right you are!" Francis chuckled, "How very right you are!"

As Brother Leo followed the little brother down the bank to get a drink of water he wondered to himself, 'How do we know the will of God?'

Brother Francis knelt and scooped up water to drink until he was no longer thirsty. Then, splashing his face and neck, he turned to Brother Leo, who was also finished. "The will of God is always the path, the decision, the act, the thought, the word and the deed that will lead us closest to God," Francis said, "and bring him the greater glory."

Brother Leo felt the color come up in his neck. Again Brother Francis of Assisi had read his thoughts. It was a startling gift. But Brother Leo was glad, because the answers to many of his questions came through Brother Francis' knowing his heart.

'And with many answers, one day,' Brother Leo thought, 'I pray I shall have at least a little wisdom.'

"Oh, you will," Brother Francis said, as if Brother Leo had spoken aloud. Then he smiled, a twinkle in his dark eyes. "With the great virtue of fear of God and love for his will, he will lead you to know Queen Wisdom and her sister Holy Simplicity."

So the two little brothers continued on the long dusty road toward the town of Spoleto to preach the Holy Word of God, to learn to find Queen Wisdom by walking with her sister Holy Simplicity.

"Dear Brother

THE
Reward
of the
PLOUGHED
Field

Francis, I could hardly wait to get back here!" Brother Polino wrung his hands, excitement trembling in his round body as he spoke. "There is a place hidden in the foothills of the Apennine Mountains, a holy place, abandoned," he panted, trying to talk and catch his breath at the same time. "It would be the perfect place for a hermitage, a place of prayer, solitude. Just like you love, and it . . ."

"Stop, stop!" Brother Francis laughed, throwing back his dark head. "Catch your breath, good Brother, and start from the beginning."

Brother Polino breathed hard for a full ten breaths. Slowly, his heart slowed and breathing became easier. He grinned. His round face lit up with the expression.

"You must have run the last mile or two!" Brother Francis said, a smile still on his eager face. "What have you discovered?"

"It is a wondrous thing!" Brother Polino clasped his stubby-fingered hands under his chin. Squinting his eyes, he licked his lips and began, "While I was at Fabriano preaching the Holy Word, we heard of some nuns who had moved from a hidden convent in the foothills." Brother Polino's voice quivered with excitement. "The nunnery is in ruins now, they said, but the church, a small gem dedicated to the Blessed Virgin Mother of Jesus, is still intact!" Brother Polino's nostrils opened wide. "The nuns said we could have it, gave me a paper." He lifted his face to the sky. It was as if he could already smell the sweet scents lingering in those special places dedicated to prayer.

"Is it a suitable place for a house of brothers?" Rising to his feet, Brother Francis studied Brother Polino closely.

"I suppose so," Brother Polino said, coming out of his trance and suddenly shrugging. "We have to go to see it."

Nodding, Brother Francis knit his brows thoughtfully. Patting Brother Polino's arm, he said, "We must start at once! Did the nuns give you directions?"

"Of course, yes." Brother Polino hurried to the door. "Directions of a sort."

Hearing that, Brother Francis raised his hands to heaven, his face shining with thankfulness. "Just think, little Brother, a place to start reviving dedication to our Lord's Blessed Mother." Ushering Brother Polino ahead of him, he smiled delightedly. "So many people have forgotten how she gave us our Beloved Savior." Brother Francis paused, looking up to heaven, and said, "Oh, how much love she has for her son. And how she can teach us to love him, as she does."

With that said, Brother Francis and Brother Polino began their journey to find the deserted church and nunnery.

They had no trouble finding the foothills or the path winding through them. It was a place that could almost be said to be irresistible to pilgrims because the path was so beautiful and so very well worn, as if by many feet. The beauty of the place was not so much in the kinds of trees there or in the colors of the rocky hills, but the beauty lay in how the soft sunlight filtered through olive branches and made patterns of light and shadow on the uneven surfaces of gray rock. Between the rocks, delicate green grasses grew as if nourished by the protection from the harshest sun. All of the play of brilliance and shade contributed to an almost enchanted atmosphere in the place.

Brother Francis and Brother Polino had found it a pleasant journey. But after walking for some time, they had to admit the nuns' directions had not been clear. They were lost.

Walking steadily on the curving path, Brother Francis noticed that it wound up a sloping hill and out of sight. They came to the crest of the hill. Down below was a valley nestled between the hills. The valley was strewn with rocks. In the midst of it, a farmer toiled with an ox and plow, struggling to make furrows so that he could eventually plant his seeds.

"I think we are lost," Brother Francis sighed.

"Perhaps if we follow the path long enough . . .," Brother Polino began. But his brow was beaded with perspiration and the expression on his face said he was ready to give up, or ready to take a rest.

"Wait here, Brother, rest," Brother Francis patted his arm encouragingly. "I shall go down to that farmer and ask him how to find the little church and nunnery."

Brother Polino did not try to stop him. In fact, he was perfectly contented to sit on a rock by the path and wait. With a sigh he sat down, watching Brother Francis approach the farmer.

"Peace of the Lord Jesus be upon you, good farmer!" Brother Francis said when he was nearly beside the struggling farmer.

"I welcome peace, believe me," the man grunted, as the plow hit a stone and stopped him short. Bending, he dragged out a fist-sized rock and tossed it into a pile already two feet high.

"Have you heard of a little church and deserted nunnery not far from here, in these hills?" Brother Francis bent and dug out two more rocks. He carried them to the stack.

"Deserted?" the farmer, preoccupied, nodded his thanks. "Oh," he said, "the Benedictine nuns' place." The farmer nodded again, his weathered face dripping perspiration.

"Yes, yes." Squatting, Brother Francis dug out another rock. "The nuns are now in Fabriano," he said.

"Of course. I know the place." The Farmer urged his ox forward with a nudge of his stick. "Not far from here," he added between clenched teeth, as the plow struck yet another rock.

"Perhaps you could tell me how to get there," Brother Francis said, walking alongside. He bent and pulled out the rock the farmer had hit.

"Up the path a little, take the right fork. Or was it the left?" The farmer wiped the perspiration from his face on his sleeve as he spoke. "Anyway you go up the narrowest trail. It widens out and you go to the south of the large boulder until you reach the fruit grove. Beyond the grove about . . . well, a little way, is the church." The farmer shot Francis a weary look. "Pilgrims go that way, sometimes," he added, as though trying to be more helpful.

After a moment's silence, Brother Francis walked ahead of the farmer, stopped and faced him. "Maybe you can show us the way?" he asked gently.

Wiping his face with a fierce stroke of his sleeve, the farmer frowned. "What? Am I to stop ploughing and waste valuable time on you?"

"Please, dear friend. We have been walking half the day and cannot find it," Brother Francis said, holding the man's gaze.

"Then walk the other half. I have a field to plough and

not much day left to do it in." Turning aside the farmer tried to go on.

"It is a fine field," Brother Francis said after him, "and a true blessing that God has given it to you to raise food for your family."

"Given! Not given. It requires hard, backbreaking work," the farmer growled, almost under his breath.

"Surely you would like to see the church in use again, and devotion to the Blessed Mother stirring in hearts once again." Brother Francis' voice was soft, yet there was an eagerness in it that made the man turn and look at him.

"The Blessed Virgin has helped us through many hard times," the farmer said, his face softening. Yet still, his eyes swept over the unploughed field. Reluctance was heavy in his heart.

"I promise you, good brother, you will lose nothing if you help us."

Inhaling a long slow breath, the farmer's eyebrows went up. He said, "Well, I guess it wouldn't take that long." Taking off the plough straps, he led the ox to the water and tethered it in the shade. "Let's not delay. I have to get back to plough, set my seed in the ground and water before sunset."

"Very well!" Brother Francis rushed ahead of the farmer. "Come on, Brother Polino. This good man is going to show us the way to the church!"

"He's heard of the place?" Brother Polino said, struggling to get to his feet and hurry after them.

"Yes. He says pilgrims go there often." Excitement shone in Brother Francis' eyes. Devotion to the Blessed Mother had not completely gone from the area. It was a promising sign!

The farmer led the way, wiping his hands on his

trousers. Brother Francis offered him a drink from their water flask. The farmer gladly took it. They walked for a good hour. The path turned and curved, the trees providing shade and beauty for the three men.

"See that fork?" the farmer asked, pointing. "You take the south branch and keep going until you get to the big boulder."

"Please, won't you show us?" Brother Francis begged.

"I'll never get my field planted if I take you all the way there," the man muttered. "It's all the rocks," he added, answering the questioning look in Brother Polino's eyes. "So many rocks I have to keep stopping." Throwing up his hands he said, "And now this interruption." But he motioned them on, leading them down the south fork.

"Don't worry," Brother Francis said in a soothing voice. "The Lord will reward you for your generous gift to us."

"What gift?" The farmer said over his shoulder.

"The gift of your time, of course," Brother Francis said with a cheerful smile. "Time well spent is precious in the sight of the Lord."

The farmer didn't comment, but his eyes said he thought he could use his time much better.

Finally, they came to the boulder the farmer had mentioned. It was higher than a house and white like chalk. Someone had scratched a large cross into it. Brother Francis and Brother Polino made the sign of the cross. Brother Francis paused for a moment in front of it to pray.

"That way, past the groves," the farmer said loudly, stopping.

"How far are the groves?" Brother Polino asked, his eyes worried.

Shrugging, the farmer heaved a sigh. "If I continue all the way I won't have enough time to plant, seed and water," he complained loudly, as if he had never made his objections clear.

"Then it is a lot farther?" Brother Polino asked.

"No, it is not." The farmer drew himself up. "Come on. It's just over that hill."

Together they crossed through the grove and over the hill into a small valley shaded by many beautiful trees. Nearby a creek wandered through a small weed-entangled garden. The small stone church was draped in emerald vines. The very sight of it brought quietness to each of their hearts. It was as if all the hundreds of prayers said there wafted over them in a cooling, calming breath.

Brother Polino heard Brother Francis' quick intake of breath.

"This is a holy place," the farmer said.

They walked to the little church. Though it was dusty and vines had made their way in, the church was undamaged. On the far wall, a painting of the Virgin and child was in perfect condition. The eyes of the Virgin held them, welcomed them, pulling them into the church.

"Thank you, good brother," Brother Francis whispered to the farmer, dropping to his knees.

The farmer watched him and Brother Polino for several breaths. Then, whispering a prayer for help with his fields, he made the Sign of the Cross and hurried out.

Across the little valley, over the hill, through the grove, the farmer rushed. Panting with effort, he glanced up at the sky. The sun was more than halfway down. Picking up his pace, he muttered another prayer and rushed to the white boulder. Pausing to catch his breath, he once again made the Sign of the Cross and ran on.

Finally, the farmer came to the fork in the road. With a sigh, he hurried toward the valley where his field waited.

He came out of the trees as the sun teetered on the peaks of the mountains surrounding the valley. The day was almost gone. Closing his eyes, he shook his head. "Another whole day gone," he moaned. Then, opening his eyes, he gazed at the field.

"What!" he uttered. Stumbling back, he stared, mouth wide open. His heart was pounding. He could not believe what he was seeing. The field was neatly ploughed. A low wall of stones surrounded it, as if whoever ploughed had used the stones removed from the rows to build the wall!

Rubbing his eyes, the farmer stared and stared and stared. The ox was still where he had left it and the strong sweet scent of damp earth filled the air. The field was damp. Someone had watered it!

Rushing to his pouch of seed, he found it empty! Ploughed, planted and watered. The work had been accomplished by some unseen hand.

"Some unseen divine hand," the farmer breathed, his heartbeat still uneven from the astonishment. Turning toward the little church, he thought he heard a low melodic voice carried on the twilight breeze.

"You are our hope,
    You are our faith, You are our charity,
    You are all our sweetness, You are our eternal life:
    Great and wonderful Lord, Almighty God, Merciful
        Savior."*

The man wept for joy. He had been rewarded for the gift of his time. And with the lilting voice of Brother Francis the farmer sang, "God almighty, merciful savior, merciful savior, merciful savior," over and over again.

---

* These words are from Saint Francis' "The Praises of God."

"Why are the people

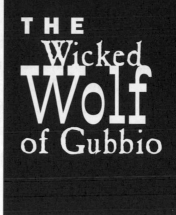

of Gubbio in such a hurry to get off the streets?" Brother Francis asked, as he lowered his very thin form to the chair his friend offered.

"Ah, that is a long story," Peruchio said in a low voice. He was a big man. He had powerful hands, a large shaggy head and great wide shoulders. With all the power and strength Brother Francis saw in him, he was surprised to see Peruchio roll those massive shoulders as if to rid himself of a shudder of dread.

Before Peruchio could go on, two merchants hurried by his house. Both of them seemed out of breath. Their faces were splotchy and their eyes wide. Glancing over their shoulders, they rattled by. Their swords and knives clanking loudly against bags of items they brought back from another town.

"Why are they carrying so many weapons?" Brother Francis wondered aloud. It looked as if they were going off to war or to a battle. Turning his liquid ebony eyes to Peruchio questioningly, he waited.

"Let me make certain the door is closed," Peruchio said, licking his lips and rubbing his big hands together. Then he clumped to the door and pushed a heavy bar down across it.

"It is still daylight, good Peruchio," Brother Francis smiled, trying to sound reassuring. "What is so fearful you are locking your wife and children into the house?"

Peruchio grinned, suddenly embarrassed. He sat down across from the smaller man. "You wouldn't think one wolf could spread such terror in a whole town," Peruchio's low voice rumbled, fear and anger trembling in it.

"A wolf!" Brother Francis said. Then he smiled as Peruchio's wife brought them both cool cups of fresh grape juice. Nodding his thanks, he sipped a little. He knew better than to try to hurry the big peasant man. Peruchio was not a man who said much usually. And so, the fact that he wanted to talk about this wolf was important. Brother Francis' fine nostrils flared. It hurt him to see Peruchio frightened. What would, what could frighten such a man? Peruchio was large, strong and courageous. Brother Francis remembered a time when the man wrestled two thieves to the ground by himself! And the thieves had knives!

No, Peruchio was no coward. And he was a man of faith. So what was it that bothered him?

As if the big man heard the quiet inner dialogue of the little brother, he cleared his throat. "No one knows where it came from or where it hides," he began, his broad face draining of color. "This wolf is so large . . ." Spreading his hands, he tried to show a size. "It is so large two of the finest hounds owned by the richest merchant in Gubbio, were killed and eaten by it with little or no trouble!"

"And the wolf has been killing livestock?" Brother Francis asked, finishing his juice and folding his hands.

"Livestock, yes, and people," Peruchio rose and brought a large staff from the corner. One end of it was broken. "It is so rabid with hunger it will kill anyone and any animal that goes outside the city gates." Holding out the staff for the brother to see, he said, "Seven of us went after it when it killed a woman and her two-year-old daughter." Rolling the sleeve of his shirt up and opening a bandage he showed Brother Francis a terrible wound. At least eight inches long, it was also very deep. Worse yet, a great hunk of flesh was missing! The herbs under the bandage were slow in helping it heal.

"Hardly anyone dares go outside the gates," Peruchio said rewrapping his arm. "Even with our weapons two men were killed. It is a terrible creature."

"Has it come into the city?" Brother Francis looked from Peruchio to his wife and back.

"No. The gates are kept closed," Peruckio replied. "Guards are posted day and night." After a short pause he continued, "This hideous wolf is choking the city."

Immediately wanting to put his arms around them both to comfort them and to wipe away the terror from their eyes, Brother Francis got to his feet. With a deep breath he said, "My dear friends, I must see this terrible wolf."

"No!" Peruchio slapped his open hand down on the wooden table with a crash! "I won't allow it. The wolf will kill and eat you!"

"You cannot let it go on forever," Brother Francis said gently.

"Seven strong men could not kill it!" Peruchio's voice broke, his eyes filling with tears. "Surely one small brother will hardly be a mouthful."

"Please, dear brother, please don't go," Peruchio's wife pleaded. "We would feel terrible if you were killed. Our hearts would be broken."

Brother Francis grew very quiet. What loving friends. Surely he could not just let the creature continue its hideous rampage. Pity filled his heart until he thought it would burst. "I must go!" he said suddenly.

"No, no, no," Peruchio shook his large head, putting his face in his hands.

"Do not be afraid for me, good Peruchio. I will put my trust in our blessed Lord Jesus Christ." Brother Francis' words silenced Peruchio and his wife. "He is the Master of all creatures, dear friends."

Inhaling a long, slow breath, Peruchio nodded. His heavy black brows lowered with worry. He said, "I will go with you."

"If you must," Brother Francis replied. "We will arm ourselves, not with shields, staves, swords or helmets, but with the Sign of the Cross."

"It is a fearful thought," Peruchio's wife protested softly. "That there will be nothing between you but your faith in God. So many have died trying to kill it." Wrapping her arms around herself she trembled. "Just the thought of its blazing yellow eyes makes me shiver in broad daylight."

"Still, we must go," Brother Francis returned firmly. "We will have our faith in the Lord. He does not fail. Remember, he makes those who believe in him walk on poisonous snakes and not be harmed. Even if we were to trample on a lion, he will protect us. And this is a wolf." Brother Francis looked at each of them, his eyes glowing with confidence.

Peruchio bowed his head. His wife grew quiet. Both were humbled by the little brother's courageous faith.

The next morning Peruchio went with Brother Francis to the gates of the city. By the time they reached them, a great many people had heard that the little brother was going out to try to stop the fierce wolf's rampage.

Peruchio and five other townsmen followed Francis on his way down the road, but when they had left the town behind, all of them but Peruchio stopped to watch from a distance, weapons shaking in their hands.

"We can't go any farther," the others said, "because the wolf is so fierce we could be attacked and killed."

"It's all right," Brother Francis assured them, his voice gentle. "Stay here. I will go find out where the wolf lives."

Peruchio gave him a worried look, and even though his heart was pounding and his knees were rattling together from fear, he went with Brother Francis.

"You climb up on the top of that big boulder, Peruchio," Brother Francis said. "See if you can see the wolf."

Sighing with relief, Peruchio climbed to the top of the big boulder, silently hoping it was high enough so that the wolf could not reach him. From there he watched the little brother and he began to pray.

As many of the people climbed into trees and onto boulders, Brother Francis started down the road. Suddenly there was a great snarling roar! The huge wolf leapt out of the bushes. His great muscles rippling, he raced toward the little brother. With his mouth wide open and his long sharp teeth shining dangerously in the morning light, he roared. In one, two, three great leaps he was almost on top of Brother Francis!

People were screaming so loudly that they could barely hear Brother Francis' words.

"In the name of the Father and of the Son and of the Holy Spirit," Brother Francis said, his eyes glimmering with fierce determination. Making the Sign of the Cross, he neither flinched or retreated.

The wolf slowed to a walk. Closing his great jaws, he paused. He licked his lips. Then raising wide yellow eyes, he looked up into the face of Brother Francis.

"Come to me, Brother Wolf," said Brother Francis, his voice neither fierce nor angry but gentle and compelling.

"In the name of our Holy Lord Jesus Christ, come to me. I command you not to harm me or anyone else."

The wolf's yellow eyes gleamed, but he did not attack Francis. Slowly, the wolf came and lowered his huge head. Lying down at Brother Francis' feet, he whined softly.

"Brother Wolf, you have done terrible things to these people. You have killed animals without mercy. But worse," Brother Francis shook his head, his eyes full of sorrow, "worse yet, you have become so bold you committed the hideous crime of killing and devouring human beings, made in the image of God."

The wolf raised his eyes. For a moment he looked into Brother Francis' dark gaze. The fierceness was gone from the wolf's eyes. A question gleamed in the yellow disks.

"You deserve to be put to death for so many horrible crimes," Brother Francis said, his voice trembling with emotion. "Everyone is right in crying out against you," he said. "Because of all these terrible things you have done, you have even become the enemy of God!"

The wolf sighed heavily, his huge body beginning to tremble.

"All the people want you to be killed, as a murderer or the worst kind of criminal would be put to death," Brother Francis cried, his voice choking in his throat. Then seeing the wolf trembling with remorse he said, "But Brother Wolf, I believe there can be peace between this city and you. I believe you are sorry."

Again the wolf lifted his head, glancing toward the city. The sound of the people gasping with fear carried to Brother Francis on the breeze.

"We must make peace, Brother Wolf," Brother Francis continued, "so they will not be harmed by you ever again." Then with a smile he added, "And when they have forgiven you all your crimes, no one will harm you either, neither humans nor dogs."

Raising its head again, the wolf stared at Brother Francis.

"Are you willing to accept these conditions?" Brother Francis asked.

Slowly the wolf's tail began to wag. Then he nodded his great head. Whispers of astonishment rose louder in the quiet day.

"Good, Brother Wolf!" Brother Francis nodded. "Since you are willing to keep this pact of peace, I promise, as long as you live, the people of Gubbio will feed you every day. You will never suffer from hunger again." Cocking his dark head Brother Francis gazed into the now calm yellow eyes. "I know all the evil you have done was because of hunger. Now you must stop."

The wolf let out a deep sigh.

"You must promise me you will never hurt any animal or man again," Brother Francis said, and slowly lowering himself to the wolf's level, he extended a thin hand to the animal. "Give me a pledge, Brother Wolf, that you will keep the promise that I ask of you."

The wolf slowly sat up. Sitting, it was taller than the little brother who was kneeling. But the wolf did not growl or snarl. Neither did it make any hostile sign. Instead, it gently lifted a large paw and placed it in the little brother's hand.

"Wonderful!" Brother Francis exclaimed. Then, gazing steadily into the large yellow eyes, he said, "Now, Brother Wolf, in the name of Jesus Christ, let us go into the town. Have no fear. You must come and make the pact of peace with me again, in front of all the people." Smiling into the wolf's worried eyes, he added, "Only then will they believe you have made the promises I have asked."

Hearing this, the wolf waited for Brother Francis to get to his feet. Then the wolf walked along beside Francis with great dignity and gentleness. Slowly they approached the people watching from a distance.

"By heaven!" Peruchio cried. "He has tamed the wolf!"

Peruchio's words rang out in the silent air. The people rushed back to the town, spreading the word so quickly a great crowd gathered at the marketplace. Men, women, children, the humble and the important all hurried to see the pact the terrible wolf would make with the gentle brother.

When Brother Francis saw the crowd, he began to speak in a strong confident voice. "Good people," he said, "God has seen fit to tame this savage wolf so you will recognize how great his mercy is!"

Some nodded their heads; others looked disbelieving. But when Brother Francis asked the wolf once again for the pledge of its paw, after stating the terms of the peace pact, many of the people were astounded. Their awe was so great Brother Francis saw they were ready to listen to God's Word. So he began to speak.

"This has been a terrible tribulation for everyone in Gubbio. Why did the Lord not stop it?" Looking from face to face, Francis went on, expecting no answer. "Because God allows these horrible things to come about due to your sins. All have sinned and have fallen short of the glory of God. But you must stop sinning. You must avoid sin at all costs. Sin kills the love of God in the soul. Sin makes the soul an unfit place for the Lord to be."

Turning to the wolf, Francis said, "This wolf had all of you in such fear for your lives you would have let your jobs be ruined. You would have neglected all your responsibilities. And the wolf can only kill your body!" After a pause, he went on, "But your soul, if you continue to sin, your soul will be in danger of worse torments, greater terror than one wolf could ever cause. To be plunged into hell would be more horrible than thousands of wolves attacking the body!"

Brother Francis could hear the sharp intake of breath. He saw the fear again on the faces of the crowd.

"Come back to the Lord. Do good. Practice your faith and do fitting penance. Then our Blessed Lord will free you from the wolf in this world. And he will free you from burning in everlasting hell fire in the next."

Brother Francis took a deep breath, letting his words sink in. "Now, Brother Wolf has promised never to harm any of you or your animals again. If you feed him the rest of his life, I will guarantee the wolf will keep his pledge. God is my witness. Do you agree to feed him every day, as much as he needs?"

"Yes," said the people, speaking almost in one voice, agreeing to the pact.

Brother Francis nodded. Then, smiling, he asked the wolf once again to give him his paw as pledge that he would not betray the trust put in him. To the amazement of all the people, Brother Wolf again made the paw pledge, wagging his thick tail. The crowd was so filled with excitement and awe, the people began to shout for joy!

"Praised be Jesus Christ now and forever!" Peruchio yelled, raising his thick arms to heaven.

"Amen. Amen. Amen," the people answered in a roar of enthusiasm. Suddenly they were dancing, singing, cheering and embracing. They exclaimed the goodness of God's mercy in that he would send the holy little Brother Francis to free them from the wicked wolf and to save them from the scourge of hell.

Peace came back to Gubbio. From that day the wolf and the people kept the pact Brother Francis made between them. The huge wolf lived inside the city, going from door to door patiently and gently receiving all the food he desired.

Slowly the people began to love the fierce wolf. He hurt no one and no one harmed him. Even the dogs befriended him. Not a single dog ever barked at the wolf!

And Gubbio lived in peace with the wolf. He reminded them of the kindness and patience of the little brother from Assisi. Turning from their sins as the wolf turned from his evil ways, the hearts of the people in Gubbio were changed. Many souls were drawn to love God and to cherish his mercy by the taming of the wicked wolf of Gubbio.

Paulo

stretched his thin arms and yawned. Another warm summer day dawned. The village of Sant' Elia was a quiet place to live. Paulo, like many of the peasants, raised oxen and farmed for his living. So he rose early with the sun and worked very hard all day long.

"Fine weather," Paulo said, dressing and eating his breakfast of cheese, bread and milk. As he came out of his small house, he looked up toward the hills. "Peace be unto you, little Brother," he said, as he did every day since he heard that the little Brother Francis of Assisi was living at a hermitage not far away, at Fonte Colombo.

After saying his morning prayers and greeting the day, Paulo went out to let his oxen out of the pasture to graze on the wild grasses.

"God is good," Paulo said, prodding the cattle slowly. The large beasts moved out onto the path, gradually to follow it up over the hill and out of sight to where the grass was lush and thick around a large pond.

Hearing the sound of feet on the rocky road, Paulo looked up surprised. "Georgio, what's your hurry?" he laughed. The sight of the heavy man lumbering along, huffing and puffing, made Paulo grin. Then the grin slowly disappeared.

What would make Georgio run? Only something serious could accomplish this.

Shortly, Georgio stumbled to a stop. Bending over with his thick hands on his knees, he wheezed loudly. Trying to get his breath he said, "Oh, Paulo . . . oh, I . . . ran all the way." As he gasped between every few words his voice sounded like something crawling through dry grass.

"All the way from your place?" Paulo smiled again. Georgio's land lay next to his. Such a short run was hardly worth boasting about.

"No, no," Georgio waved a big hand at him and stood straight. "All the way from the village square. The farms on the other side of Sant' Elia."

"You look upset," Paulo said, brushing his own thick black hair out of his eyes and staring at Georgio's red face.

"Upset," Georgio gulped air, his cheeks splotchy, "I am . . ." Waving his arms around, he tried to think of a good word. "I am worried sick."

"Okay, okay," Paulo said, putting an arm around the bigger man's shoulders. "I just let my cattle out. Let's go back to the house and have a little wine."

"You let your oxen out!" Georgio yelled, clenching his fists. "Get them back! Hurry! Quick! Get them back!" Almost jumping up and down, Georgio's voice squeaked in his throat.

"Get them back?" Paulo stared at his friend as if he had lost his mind. "It is a beautiful day. They need to graze by the water, in the hills where it is green."

"No!" Georgio barked, looking wild-eyed. Then taking Paulo by the shoulders, he pushed him toward the house. "Okay. I'll have a quick cup of wine. Just to get my strength. But then, then I'll help you bring them back."

"Georgio, what foolishness is this? Cattle need the green grass." Paulo shook his head. "I told you I just turned them out of the fenced pasture."

"When you hear what I have to say," Georgio nodded soberly, his round cheeks jiggling with the motion, "you will change your mind and want to do as I said."

So Paulo took Georgio back to his small sod-covered house. Inside it was cool and smelled of bunches of herbs. The mints and the rosemary, the thyme and the dill gave the air an especially spicy, fresh scent. All the herbs kept the air smelling fresh, although the little house had no window.

Taking two cups, Paulo poured some wine from a jug on the wooden table. "It is still cool from the night," Paulo said sipping slowly. His dusky features lit up with a smile at the sweet taste. "Good. Drink, Georgio, refresh yourself."

Georgio sipped, then gulped the wine. Exhaling loudly as the sweet beverage brought new energy to his body, he set his cup down. "Paulo, I was at the market and heard a horrendous thing."

"Gossip? Ah, Georgio," Paulo shook his head. He did not encourage his friends or family to tell rumors or stories and he wouldn't listen to them. Paulo was a very religious man.

"No, it is not like that," Georgio said quickly, biting his lip. "Oxen, Paulo, oxen are dying."

For a moment Paulo stared as if he had not heard. Then he said, "Oxen, our cattle, ours? From what?"

"That is just the thing," Georgio grunted. Then taking a very deep breath, he said, "Some are saying it is from contaminated water. Some are saying contaminated pasture." Georgio lowered his scraggly brows.

"And my oxen drink from the water that comes from north of here," said Paulo, "the tributary that the other farmers use to water their animals."

Georgio nodded vigorously. His cheeks jiggling, breath raspy, he waited, one hand gripping his wine cup.

"How many have died?"

"I don't know," Georgio sputtered, after pouring himself more wine and taking a drink. "Four of mine already. Many to the south."

"I don't understand why we did not hear of this sooner."

"How often do we trade news at the market?" Georgio said heavily. "It is all over the place. So many oxen are stricken people are beginning to panic. They can't get their fields plowed. They do not have any animals for meat."

"You have lost four already?" Paulo stared, his eyes widening.

"Yes, four. And many of my herd are stricken. I just hope and pray they will survive." Georgio did not look very hopeful. He hung his head shaking it slowly. "If I lose too many I will starve."

Paulo corked his wine jug. Putting on his cap he turned to the door. "You are a good friend to come and tell me, Georgio."

Georgio smiled weakly.

"You are right, I had better go and get my oxen." Whistling for his dog, Paulo waved as Georgio followed him out. "Go home and tend your sick cattle. I can get mine in alone."

Nodding, Georgio waved back, shouting over the short distance, "Don't let them drink the water!"

Paulo lifted a hand to let him know he heard. Then, hurrying up the path, he followed the trail to the lush green grasses and the still pond. He had no doubts he would find all of his oxen there. It was their favorite place in the hot summer.

By noon he had gotten all his cattle back into the pasture. Throwing hay in for them, he muttered unhappily, "This kind of food won't fatten an ox." But he was more worried about the plague than he was about the weight of his oxen, so he did not let them out to graze.

He walked slowly back to his work. It was impossible to keep his mind off the plague. 'Poor Georgio,' he thought. 'He cannot afford to lose four oxen. And he could lose even more.' He did not want to think about what he would do if he lost his own. He did not have that many.

In the late afternoon, he checked on the oxen. He found three of his ten oxen lying on their sides moaning. Their breath was labored, and their big dark eyes were clouded with pain.

'They are stricken,' Paulo thought. Slowly stroking the large heads, he prayed and prayed. Then he wondered and wondered what he could do to help them. By nightfall, two more began to stumble and moan as if their bellies hurt.

Filling their water trough with clear water he had boiled, Paulo put down fresh hay. Finally, he went inside to get himself some dinner.

The house was still cool. Although the day had been warm enough to make Paulo perspire, inside it was comfortable. He left the door open so he could hear the oxen. Wiping the perspiration from his forehead with a soft cloth, he dropped heavily onto a chair.

"I am too tired to eat," he said softly. Dropping a wooden bowl of cheese, meat and milk on the floor for his dog, he sighed, "I am weary and sick at heart. Five of my ten oxen are dying, Lord." Pouring himself wine, he drank. Then he cut a piece of bread and ate it.

He was too weary to get up and get ready for bed. Instead, he put his head down across his arm and fell asleep at the table. One hand still clutched his empty cup, the other his rosary.

Just before dawn, Paulo awoke. As he opened his eyes,

he saw a tall figure surrounded by light.

'Is the house on fire?' he wondered, not understanding how it could be so bright when he had not lit a lamp.

"No, Paulo," a voice said. "The house is not on fire."

Rubbing his eyes, Paulo stared. The man was dressed in peasant's clothes, but his tunic and trousers were so white they seemed to have a light of their own. His face was kind. His eyes, dark like wells, held Paulo's attention.

"You have asked what you should do," the man nodded. At that moment Paulo knew he was speaking about the oxen and the plague. "Go to the hermitage where blessed Brother Francis is living. Ask his companion to get some water in which he has washed his hands and feet. Then sprinkle the water on your oxen. They will be cured at once."

Straightening as if someone had pricked his bottom with a pin, Paulo stood up. As Paulo rose, the stranger vanished. Making the Sign of the Cross, Paulo thanked God. Then hurrying, he left for the hermitage where Brother Francis was staying. Not once did he question the vision. He was too sure it was the answer to his prayers.

The hermitage was not far from Paulo's farm and it took no more than an hour to get there.

"Peace and all good," Brother Rufino, one of Brother Francis' companions, greeted Paulo. "What brings you here on such a fine day?"

"Ah, good Brother," Paulo said and took off his cap, smiling. "It is a fine day." Paulo hesitated.

"Go on," Brother Rufino said, suddenly concerned.

"Have you not heard about the plague that has stricken the oxen of this area?" Paulo asked, his voice rough with sorrow.

"Yes," Brother Rufino said and waved him closer to the

fire. "I heard about it when we were preaching in the village. It is a terrible thing."

Paulo nodded. Then, licking his lips, he twisted his cap. Would this brother believe he had seen a vision? Shrugging off the doubt he said, "I had a vision this morning, Brother."

"A vision?"

"Yes. In the vision the visitor answered the prayer for help I had been praying." Paulo paused trying to get his thoughts together. "You see my oxen are very ill, are dying. And I will starve if I lose them."

"I see. What did the visitor say in this vision?" Brother Rufino asked quietly.

"To come here, to this hermitage where Blessed Francis is." Paulo gestured toward the little cave a distance away where he knew the brother to be.

"And what is it you want Brother Francis to do?"

Paulo dropped his gaze to his shoes. "The visitor asked me only to get water Blessed Brother Francis had washed his hands and feet in. Then," Paulo looked back into Brother Rufino's eyes before going on, "then to sprinkle it on my stricken oxen. They will be cured at once."

Brother Rufino stared for a long time. Then he sighed, as if he were thinking very hard. Leaning forward, he whispered, "I don't want to disturb Brother Francis by telling him of the terrible plague. But I will get you the water."

Paulo smiled. "Thank you," he said, his eyes full of gratitude. He watched the brother go back to the cave with a bucket of water.

Crouching by the fire, Paulo stirred the burning sticks. The brother had believed him! What a strange vision. Clutching his rosary, he knew that Brother Rufino's belief was part of the miracle. Quivering, he prayed quietly. He could hear the voices of the brothers in the cave but he could not hear their words.

Some time ago, Georgio had told him that people were saying Blessed Brother Francis had the wounds of Jesus in his hands and feet. Paulo wondered if it were true. Then he thought, 'It has to be true. That is why I was told to bring the water from the washing of the hands and feet.' Excitement stirred in him. He was certain to see blood in the water, if it was so.

Some time later, Brother Rufino returned. "Here is the water," he said. "You may return the bucket whenever you can come back." Brother Rufino's eyes were bright, his face full of a strange happiness, almost as if he had been looking at something, or someone, very holy.

"Thank you, Brother," Paulo said humbly. "Please thank blessed Brother Francis for me." Hurrying away, he returned to his house.

As he neared his house he could hear the soft moaning of the stricken oxen. His heart ached. "God willing, this water will relieve their suffering," he prayed.

Dipping a clean cloth into the bucket, he saw that the water was just the slightest bit pink, as if from blood! The wounds, the brother did have the wounds. Hurrying to the oxen his chest grew tight as he saw them lying on their sides. Their breath heaving, their mouths open, he could see they were dying.

But as the water touched them, they shivered. Then suddenly they lunged to their feet, lowing in booming voices! Right before Paulo's eyes their bodies seemed to fill out, their eyes cleared. They rumbled toward the water troughs to quench their thirst. One by one, the five oxen came to their feet. Suddenly they were well! The terrible sickness that had made them suffer was gone!

"God be praised!" Paulo cried, crossing himself with his rosary. Gathering all his strength, he ran to Georgio's, carrying the bucket of water. By the grace of God, Georgio's dying oxen were also cured! Then, pouring the last of the water into the pond from which the oxen drank, both men prayed that many other oxen would be spared from the terrible plague.

Paulo felt as if he were walking on clouds. In thanksgiving, he prayed many extra rosaries. He made a little shrine in the corner of his house where he had seen the vision. And when he prayed there, he thanked God with all his enthusiasm.

Then he asked the good Lord to bless little Brother Francis, through whose innocent holiness the stricken oxen had been cured.

"There have

been so many joining our brother-hood this year it almost seems like a miracle," Brother Rufino said, scratching his red beard and sighing.

THE Obedient Birds

"Yes, indeed," Brother Antonio agreed, walking easily beside the shorter brother. He slowed down to match the other man's stride. "It is truly a miracle from God that so many want to leave the world," Brother Antonio said enthusiastically. The air was very warm, but the abundance of reeds and brush and trees made it smell fresh and clean.

"Look at all those birds," Brother Rufino changed the subject, pointing to a great flock of birds flying to the damp land nearby.

"Yes! Look at them!" Brother Francis stopped short in his tracks. Because Francis was walking a little ahead, Brother Antonio almost ran into his back. "Doves, crows, daws, sparrows," Brother Francis continued, his smile seeming to grow by the moment.

Brother Rufino laughed softly, suddenly excited by the birds, too. "So many different kinds, and all of them seem to be gathering to the same spot."

"There must be water and a lot of food nearby," Brother Antonio chimed in. He watched Brother Francis with a look of respect and great affection on his long face. "The birds make me think of how quickly our brotherhood has grown."

"Especially the hooded larks!" Brother Francis whispered as if he were afraid the flock of birds would fly away.

"Do you see them?"

"Yes, I see them," Brother Rufino pointed excitedly as he spoke.

"They remind me of little monks in their cowls or nuns in their habits," said Brother Francis, his face lit with joy. He watched the birds, not daring to move lest he cause them to fly in some direction they did not intend. He said, "See how humbly and how diligently our brothers the birds go about their little lives!" Smiling with great tenderness, he left the road to go closer.

Moving eagerly toward the variety of birds on bushes, reeds and in trees, Francis talked to them, saying, "Dear little brothers, you have been very busy today. You have been collecting your food and tending your young just as God intended you to do."

As he approached, Francis was delighted to see that the birds did not rise in flight. Instead, they flitted closer so that they brushed his bare ankles and the hem of his robe with their feathers.

"The peace of the Lord Jesus be upon you, my brother birds," Brother Francis cried in delight. Then, lowering his voice, he cocked his head and said, "Please stay a little and listen to the Word of God. For my companions and I are on a long pilgrimage, preaching his Word to everyone who will listen."

As Brother Francis spoke, the birds hopped closer. Others flew from the trees, gathering near. Even more flew to the ground, each bird cocking and turning its head to look at him with bright liquid eyes. As though they were listening, all of them seemed to grow quiet. The cheeping, chirping and tweeting died to the soft rustle of feathers and feet as they settled down. Finally, there was only the sighing of the wind in the reeds and the rustle of the leaves and branches, as more birds descended in front of the little brother.

Inhaling a short breath, Brother Francis held out his hands to the great number of birds. "My brothers, do not let a day pass that you do not praise your Creator with all your little hearts. Love him. Always love him!" he cried. Even though his voice was full of enthusiasm and rose up over the birds, none of them flew away or seemed to be startled.

Brother Antonio and Brother Rufino watched in astonishment, clasping their hands in front of them.

"Why should you love your Creator so much?" Brother Francis asked the birds, looking from one to another. Cocking his dark head, he answered his own question. "You must love him because he gave you feathers to clothe you. And such beautiful feathers! From the softest grays, to inky blacks." Brother Francis gazed to the heavens and said reverently, "And all the wonderful colors and patterns between."

Then looking back at the vast array of birds, he said, "But that is not the only reason you should praise him. Praise him because he provides you with all that is necessary to live food, water and the amazing ability to fly!" Brother Francis laughed softly, as two sparrows burst from the ground and lit on his shoulder.

"Yes, Brother Birds, God made you noble among creatures by blessing you with the purity of the air." Then cocking his head again, he concluded, "And though you neither sow nor reap, he protects you and cares for you without your ever asking!"

Clasping his hands in front of him, Brother Francis gazed up into the heavens and said, "He has given you wings like angels and songs to praise him like the heavenly choirs! So do not neglect the giving of praise to him in the glorious sounds of your voices!"

With those words, Brother Francis gazed in wonder as the birds began to sing, to twitter, cheep, chirp, caw, each making the sounds the Lord gave them for their very own. Opening and closing their wings, bowing and rising, it seemed the whole great number of them were doing exactly as Brother Francis had instructed, praising God with their voices!

What a wonderful sound it made, a rousing symphony of song, the different sounds miraculously intertwining in a beautiful melody. To the two brothers watching, it seemed a heavenly choir all its own. Brother Francis' delighted laughter seemed to add to it, to mingle with the great chorus of voices.

Raising his hands, Brother Francis asked the good Lord's blessing on the great flock of birds.

"Now you may go!" Francis cried, making the Sign of the Cross over them. "But do not forget the goodness of God!" As his words died into the silence, the birds rose, not in a great cluttered crowd but in four distinct groups.

As they shot into the air, the four groups formed a cross, hovering for a few breathtaking moments above the ground. And then they parted, each group flying in a different direction—one to the north, one to the west, one to the south and one to the east!

Brother Francis stood motionless, his face lifted to the heavens, contemplating the strange and wondrous formation. Then, dropping his chin, he turned and made his way back to his companions.

"A miracle," Brother Rufino exclaimed, as Brother Francis joined them.

"A divine wonder," Brother Antonio murmured, still in

awe of the obedient birds.

"A message," Brother Francis said thoughtfully.

Brother Rufino and Brother Antonio fell into step, one on each side of Brother Francis, both keeping very quiet. Their hearts raced. Their breathing became hurried. Was it truly a message from God?

"It is a blessed miracle that all creatures venerate our good God," Brother Francis began. "It humbles me, and should humble all men to see such devotion in the simple creatures of the Lord."

Brother Rufino nodded. Brother Antonio sighed, his heart still full of amazement.

"I should have preached to Brother Birds a long time ago," Brother Francis scolded himself humbly. "After all, the Word of God is the food of creation. It makes all things alive." Nodding, he mentally made a note not to neglect God's creatures when he went out to preach.

"In fact, that is God's message," he said, turning back and gazing at the spot where the birds had formed a cross in the air. Staring as if he could still see it, he caught his breath and cried, "Preach the Word of God in season, out of season, here, there, to the north, to the south, to the east and to the west!" Pausing to get his breath, he finished in a reverent whisper. "Preach the gospel, good brothers, to all creatures, invoking the holy name of Jesus so all may praise it."

With that, he turned back and continued the journey. Brother Rufino glanced at Brother Angelo. Both brothers smiled.

It was a miracle. It was a divine wonder and a message to both men as well. It was the miracle of the little poor man's example and the divine wonder of the obedience of Brother Birds to God's Word through Brother Francis.

Finally, there was the message. Both brothers could easily see it was from God, for it said that all the world should praise and love their Creator daily, especially mankind, whom he created in his marvelous image.

So Brother Francis and his companions continued on their pilgrimage to preach the Word of God. But from then on they preached to all birds, animals, reptiles and to all living things, especially to humankind.

Brother Francis made it his intention to send brothers to preach the Word of God in all four directions of the world. To the north, to the south, to the east and to the west! They went everywhere! To this day they proclaim, "Let the holy name of Jesus be praised!"

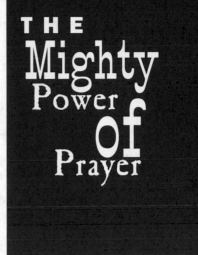

"Spoleto has

a good many people," Brother Tebaldo said thoughtfully. "What should it matter that one man, Master Jubel, refuses to give alms to any of our brothers?"

Brother Andrew sighed heavily. "It seems this Master Jubel does not just refuse to give alms. It seems he hates us."

Brother Tebaldo raised his eyebrows. "We are going into his region to preach and to beg today. Why don't we pray about this?"

"Pray all you like," Brother Andrew said reluctantly. "But watch out. I tell you this man hates our brotherhood. And he makes it no secret."

Brother Tebaldo nodded, but he smiled nonetheless. With a small group of brothers it was easy to beg enough for their house. But with so many joining them, it took longer to get enough to go around. Still, their loving natures and the love they tried to have for God usually showed. They softened people's hearts and they gave.

So with light hearts and great hope in God's mercy, the brothers still went out to get what monies and food they could from those who were touched by God's mercy to give. They went as Brother Francis taught them, putting all their trust in God. They accepted joyfully whatever God inspired others to bless them with.

"It is so easy to thank God when our alms bowls fill up with coins and bread. Or when a merchant gives a block of cheese or a sack of biscuits," Brother Tebaldo said, walking with a spring in his stride. "We can all smile and be thankful."

"How true," Brother Thomas said. "When we are blessed, each step toward home seems light and cheerful, even after miles and miles of walking."

Brother Tebaldo wore what appeared to be a satisfied smile.

"It is not so easy to accept the hardships, or the days when no one will listen to our words," Brother Thomas added, in spite of Brother Tebaldo's happy smile. "It is even worse when people throw rotten vegetables at us, or when they call us mad or spit on us."

Brother Tebaldo frowned. "Yes, it is harder to smile and thank God for those things. But we still have to try to be cheerful. We still have to try to accept the joy, as Brother Francis shows us by his example."

"How true!" Brother Thomas said softly. "I have seen our Brother Francis kicked, beaten and spit upon. He not only smiles but wishes the attacker the blessings of God!"

Brother Tebaldo nodded, his smile back, but not so carefree now. He had a sense of uneasiness, as if Brother Thomas's words were a warning of what to expect today in Spoleto.

Master Jubel owned one of the finest stone houses in Spoleto. It was huge. It took many servants and a lot of money to maintain. Master Jubel was a rich merchant. When he wasn't away trading his goods, he was home counting his money. He held on to his money tightly and rarely gave anything away.

Because he was a large man with much money, Master Jubel was used to getting his way. He had a loud bellowing voice and he used it to his best advantage. He wore the finest clothes and ate the finest food. But he did not spare one coin for the poor. Neither did he give the beggars the leavings from his tables. Instead, he claimed the stray dogs were more worthy!

Though hard-hearted, Master Jubel was prosperous. So many people in Spoleto listened to him and wanted to be counted as his friends. But Master Jubel was loyal to none but himself. And, of course, to any job or transaction that would increase his fortune.

So there was little chance he would give the brothers any coins or food. Whenever he heard the voices of the brothers begging food and alms, Master Jubel would become furious. The bright summer day Brother Tibaldo and his companions had chosen for begging in Spoleto was to be no exception.

Rushing to his door, Master Jubel threw it open and stared at the small group.

"May the Lord give you peace and bless you!" Brother Tibaldo said. Though his voice and face were cheerful, his knees were knocking together under his robe.

"I have all the peace I want!" Master Jubel's face was red with anger. "Get off my street. How dare you beg here?"

"Please sir, won't you give us a coin or a bit of bread? God loves a cheerful giver," Brother Tibaldo said, his smile fixed, his eyes wary.

"I'll give you a gift," Master Jubel blustered, "and very, very cheerfully." Master Jubel ducked back inside for a moment to retrieve a chamber pot that had not been emptied and was brimming full. He tossed it onto the brothers, yelling, "Here's a little gift for all of you!" The pot hit Brother Tibaldo square in the face.

"Yuck," said Brother Tibaldo, sputtering and wiping his face. He dropped his bowl and staggered away. The other brothers scattered with a torrent of cries of alarm.

"Don't beg on my street, worthless imbeciles," Master Jubel yelled over the noise with a satisfied smirk.

Hurrying away, the brothers helped Brother Tibaldo around the corner. The curses and insults Master Jubel yelled after them followed them like a swarm of flies.

"Are you all right?" Brother Thomas asked, worry in his green eyes.

"My eyes are burning and I reek," Brother Tibaldo said sullenly. He did not feel very much like thanking God for that gift.

"Thank God it wasn't poison or something worse," Brother Thomas murmured.

"What could be worse?" Brother Tibaldo mumbled under his breath, wishing he had never come down the street where Master Jubel lived.

"What a hateful man," another brother said softly.

"Why? Why does he hate us so much?" Brother Tibaldo said suddenly, hurt filling his voice and eyes. "And how are we supposed to show a good example to someone who acts as he does?"

"We . . . we must pray for him," Brother Thomas said with a heavy sigh. They continued down the street somewhat subdued. Even their songs held a hint of sorrow. But they could not help this after Master Jubel shamed them as he did.

By the end of the day, they had barely a few coins. Only the dry, crusty end of a loaf of bread had been given to them. They returned home very downhearted.

Eating a very sparse dinner, the growling of their stomachs made them feel more like failures.

"Why are we so full of sadness tonight?" Brother Francis asked, after returning from preaching.

Slowly, Brother Andrew began to tell him about the wicked rich man. Brother Francis listened. His head cocked thoughtfully, he nodded.

"He not only never gives us alms," Brother Andrew said with indignation, "he curses us and as he did today, he thinks up the most humiliating and shameful acts to commit against us."

"Why, Brother Francis, does he hate us so much?" Brother Tibaldo asked mournfully.

Brother Francis looked from one to the other, considering all that had been said. "Has this been going on long?" he asked.

"Many months, Brother," Brother Andrew said vigorously. "Even though we can see no reason for him to hate us, his hatred seems to be worse every time we see him."

"And he is a very rich man?"

"Very rich," Brother Tibaldo said sorrowfully. "I worry for his soul."

"Yes, yes, so do I," Brother Francis said seriously. Then after a long prayerful pause, he said, "Maybe Master Jubel is just not able to appreciate the life God has given us."

"He thinks we are worthless," Brother Andrew moaned. "He has said so many times."

"He says we should not beg, especially on his street," Brother Thomas added.

"I am worried he will become violent," Brother Tibaldo said in a frightened whisper.

"We must pray for him," said Francis. "We must beg the Lord to open his eyes. We must ask the Lord to lead him into the ways of kindness and generosity so that his heart will not stay bitter."

Brother Francis drew a long slow breath, looking from one to the other of the brothers. Francis' thin features suddenly lit up. It was as if an idea was given to him by God, for the light of his face was so bright it made the candle flames seem dim.

"Let each and every one of us begin to pray at once and every day for this poor sinner," said Francis. His nostrils flaring with the excitement of prayer, he went on, "Brother Andrew, you shall go to Master Jubel's street every day. Only you. You will go to his very door and beg from him some coin or bit of food." Then, raising a finger Francis looked into Brother Andrew's eyes before he could protest. "You must not give up. Pray, beg, pray, beg, until you have gotten from this man, something, however small. Then come home."

Brother Andrew stared. "Me?" he asked.

Smiling, Brother Francis said, "Yes, dear Brother, you. You are the first one who noticed this man's hatred. Since you are in charge of our food and alms, you will go. But only you."

"By myself?" Brother Andrew groaned, in disbelief.

"Oh no," Brother Francis said, shaking his dark head. "Take our Lord with you in your heart and in your head."

For several moments, Brother Andrew drew long breaths and fought the desire to protest. But he could not. Holy obedience. No, he would say nothing more. He would have to go. So, receiving Brother Francis' blessing, he left early the next morning, carrying his begging bowl in his hand, and the Lord in his heart and his head.

When he left, the brothers began to pray.

"Please, have mercy on a poor brother and give a coin or bit of bread," Brother Andrew cried, just below Master Jubel's window. Hoping his voice didn't shake too much, he smiled.

The window snapped open. The large face of Master

Jubel poked out. "Get out of here," he yelled. Bending over out of sight, he disappeared for a moment.

Suspecting some mischief, Brother Andrew moved across the street from the window. A shower of dirty water splashed down where he had been. The shutter slammed with a crash.

Brother Andrew flinched. What was he going to do? "Lord I don't know how to touch this man," he said, praying quietly, and made the Sign of the Cross and went over to the door. "For the sake of the Lord's mercy, won't you give a bit of bread?" he cried out, hammering the door with one fist.

"Get lost!" the muffled voice grew louder. "Get away from my house before I . . ." The door jerked open.

Brother Andrew's eyebrows flew up! His fist was still poised to knock but it hovered in front of Master Jubel's chest. Brother Andrew smiled apologetically. "We are just poor brothers doing the work of God," he said. "Please, Master Jubel, won't you give us a little food? God will bless you." Brother Andrew tried not to flinch as the man clenched his big hands into fists.

"Curse you, leeches," Master Jubel screamed into his face. "You want my hard-earned bread for nothing! You can go to the devil!"

Raising a fist, Master Jubel stood for the length of five labored breaths poised as if he would smash Brother Andrew's face. Then suddenly he turned away, slamming the door.

Brother Andrew stood motionless. His whole body was quivering with fear. Did he dare persist? But how did he dare give up? Holy obedience made it impossible for him to leave until he had something, no matter how small.

What if Master Jubel came out with a sword? Terrible

visions of being stabbed, beaten and thrown into the stone street rolled through Brother Andrew's head. "Stop. I must stop thinking like this," he said, compressing his lips together. "Yes, I am afraid. But I have the Lord in my heart and in my head. I will pray for an idea."

Moving away, Brother Andrew walked the length of Master Jubel's fine house. His lips moving in prayer, he hoped for an idea. "Remember, the brothers are supporting you with prayer," he said to himself, which made him feel a little better. What would they be doing? Suddenly he remembered how Brother Francis loved to sing. And he began to sing softly. He sang God's praises and paced the length of the house and back. When he got to the door, he paused and knocked lightly, saying, "A bit of bread for the love of Jesus?"

Over and over, back and forth, hour after hour until day became dusk he repeated this action. As he was passing the door for the hundredth time, it flew open before he could rap. Stumbling back, he expected to see Master Jubel with a sword in his hand.

It was Master Jubel, and he did have something in his hand. But it was something small. He lifted his clenched fist and threw it at Brother Andrew with all his might. It struck him right in the forehead and bounced off. Then with a string of curses on his lips Master Jubel screamed, "Now go away!"

Brother Andrew stood frozen as the sound of the door crashing back into place battered him. Turning his head, he stared at the object. Slowly a smile spread over his long features. It was a very small piece of bread. "Praised and thanked be our Lord Jesus Christ," he whispered, bending to pick it up.

With great joy, Brother Andrew carried the bit of bread

back to the house and the other brothers.

"May the holy name of Jesus be praised forever more!" he said, presenting the bread to Brother Francis with tears in his eyes. "A bit of bread from Master Jubel's fist into my face!"

"God works in wonderful ways!" Brother Francis said reverently, taking the bread.

Gathering all the brothers of the whole house together Francis said, "Let each brother say three Our Fathers and pray for this sinner, Master Jubel. Pray that God may soften his heart, open his mind and cleanse his soul, so that he can walk in the will of God. Then he will be able to do the good God requires of him and not be so attached to his riches." With that, he gave each brother a tiny morsel of the bit of bread.

The brothers sat down together around the table to eat the morsels as their supper. Slowly, reverently, they each prayed and ate. There was such a quiet in the house a person could have heard the fleas running on a dog, had there been a dog present.

Brother Francis sat, eyes closed, listening to the silence that followed all those Our Fathers.

Suddenly there was a banging on the door. "Open up!" Master Jubel's voice boomed out of the dark. "Pleeeeease, open up!"

Brother Andrew rose and hurriedly opened the door. Rushing in, Master Jubel stared wildly from brother to brother.

Brother Francis rose, studying the man's face. Joy beamed from Brother Francis' dark eyes as he waited.

With three lumbering strides Master Jubel threw himself on the floor, gripping the little Brother Francis' legs and weeping inconsolably.

"Forgive me, please, forgive me," the man sobbed.

Stroking the man's large head, Brother Francis gazed down at him with kind eyes.

The brothers stood silently, their mouths open in amazement.

"Please, please, forgive me," Master Jubel continued looking from face to face as he spoke. "I have been so cruel, so hateful, so blind." He sniffed, his cheeks trembling. "All day I was in a rage because the brother would not go away." Looking at Brother Andrew, he choked. "Then I . . . I threw the bread at him, and he smiled." Master Jubel wiped tears away but they kept coming. "Then I realized, each time the brother asked for food, he was asking for the love of Jesus, asking me to show my love for God . . ." He choked again. "And all I gave was . . . was . . ." He held up a huge hand. "A tiny, insignificant, shameful morsel." Sobbing loudly, Master Jubel squeezed his eyes closed.

"God has given us this life," Brother Francis said softly. "He leads us, he guides us, and it is he who touches the hearts of those who give." Smiling, Brother Francis pulled Master Jubel to his feet. "You have been touched by God, my dear friend."

When he heard Brother Francis calling him friend, Master Jubel wept even more vehemently.

"All is forgiven," Brother Francis said gently, putting an arm around the man's great shoulders. "Please, Master Jubel, join us for supper." Smiling and meeting the taller man's eyes he added, "All we have is a bit of bread. But it is bread blessed by the power and mercy of God's touch."

Master Jubel trembled at the words. But a smile came to his eyes, and he said, "I will bring bread and meat and cheese and wine and . . ."

Throwing his head back, Brother Francis began to

laugh. "Thank you, thank you, dear brother. Tonight let us just feast upon the new friendship that God has given us!"

Master Jubel grinned. Then he, too, laughed, the brothers joining in merrily and with great relief.

From that moment on, Master Jubel was a changed man, a humbled man, a true friend to the brothers of Brother Francis' little house. And Master Jubel became a generous supporter of God's little poor men. By doing so, he, too, showed his growing love for our merciful Savior Jesus Christ.

"The hermitage

you are asking about is a long way up the hill." The peasant man stared at Brother Francis as he spoke. "You look too frail to make such a journey."

"Do you know the way?" Brother Francis asked, not at all discouraged by the man's open criticism. He looked around the stable the man had been cleaning.

"Of course I know the way," the man said, patting his chest. "I have been taking pilgrims up to the hermitage for years."

"Good!" Brother Francis said. "But you are right about me not being strong. In fact, I have been quite ill."

"Then you better not try to make the trip," the man said, turning away with a frown. "After all it is a long hard journey. Sometimes even I suffer going up there."

"Ah, I see," Brother Francis sighed. Then slowly a smile lit his lean face. "Maybe you will let me use your donkey."

The man paused in his work. Thinking about it, he patted the donkey's rump. "He's a sturdy animal."

"Has he been up there before?"

"Yes, now that I think about it. A while ago, I lent him to a pilgrim whose leg was bad." Then, inhaling a deep breath, the man smiled. "Okay. Giovanni is not a hard-hearted man," he said, pointing to himself. "I'll feed him, give him water and early tomorrow I will take you up to the little hermitage."

"Wonderful!" Brother Francis said. "The good Lord will

bless you abundantly for your kindness."

Giovanni just smiled. He knew Brother Francis had no money and he asked none. But then, what did a poor beggar know about God's blessings? Laughing softly to himself, he watched Brother Francis go back to the little shelter by the well in the center of town.

"If that is the so-called holy Brother Francis from Assisi," he said to himself, "he doesn't look very impressive." Wiping his hands on his trousers, he shook his head. "In fact," he murmured to the donkey, "he looks like he is about ready to fall apart." Staring after Brother Francis, he rubbed the donkey's nose. "He is going to have to do something really amazing to bring God's blessing down," he muttered, picking up his shovel. "He's so skinny you can almost see through him. It's a good thing he is going to ride." Shaking his head again, he went back to his house to prepare food for the morning. "He's going to have to do something really fantastic to convince me he loves God like people claim he does."

The peasant man, Giovanni, finished his preparations for the next day. When he went to sleep he was still very set against the poor beggar he was going to take up the mountain the next day.

Brother Francis and Giovanni left early, before the sun came up. The dew was still on the grass. It trembled and sparkled as the sun began to shine over the tops of the mountains. Twinkling like thousands of sequins over the grass and leaves, the sparkling dew gave Giovanni a sense of unreality. It was almost as if they began their journey in another world.

But as the sun rose higher, the dew vanished. Like magic the glistening world of beauty was gone. In its place, the scraggly clumps of grass and the gray-green foliage looked drab and uninteresting.

"It is going to be hot," Giovanni said, leading the donkey with Brother Francis riding on it.

The little brother's eyes were closed. Opening them, he glanced at the sky, a cloudless expanse of baby blue cupping the earth. The brown and gray mounds of hills rose up to meet the sky, creating the impression of earthenwater swelling to make waves. "Beautiful," he murmured.

Giovanni shot a look skyward and frowned. Beautiful? He thinks the heat is beautiful. Already perspiration stood out on Giovanni's wide brow.

There was no shade going up the steep mountain path. There were boulder after boulder piled one on the other with barely any earth between them. What little soil had accumulated was crowded with scraggly gray grasses. Some bushes grew here and there, but there was so little water they were thin and pitifully leafless.

Though Giovanni was strong, he began to feel the heat by early afternoon. Not only was the sun pounding down on his head like hammer blows, the rocks gave off waves of heat. Giovanni panted, glancing up at Brother Francis, "Do you have any water, little Brother?"

Brother Francis sighed. "No, I'm sorry, good Giovanni, I have nothing to carry it in," he said. "I am afraid I gave my water jug to a beggar."

'Foolishness,' Giovanni thought. But he said nothing.

Giovanni nodded. 'Of course,' he thought, 'this man is a poor pilgrim. Why did I not think of water?' Glancing up at the brother, he lowered his eyebrows, puzzled. Brother Francis was not at all sweaty. His thin face was turned down. His eyes were closed. Giovanni could see no perspiration running off of him.

Blowing air out of his nostrils noisily, Giovanni wiped

his face on his sleeve. Still the path climbed up the mountain. Steeper and steeper it became, waves of heat coming from the rocks. Still the sun glared down from the sky, its heat punishing Giovanni terribly.

Giovanni's throat seemed dry as sandpaper. His tongue stuck to the roof of his mouth. His clothes were soaked with perspiration. When he swallowed it was like a rock rolling down his dry throat. And every step he took, he felt his knees would give out. Panting heavily, he paused on the trail.

"What is the matter Giovanni?" Brother Francis asked, opening his eyes and staring.

"I . . . I . . . can't go on," Giovanni gasped, sinking to his knees.

Brother Francis straightened slowly. "Isn't there any water on the way to the hermitage?" he asked, worry lining his thin cheeks.

"No, no. But I must have water," Giovanni swayed, clutching his head. "My head, my throat . . . Please, Brother Francis, please, water . . ."

Sliding off the donkey, Brother Francis held Giovanni's shoulders. "Dear Giovanni, I have no water. We must go on until we get to the hermitage where there is water."

"No, I can't," Giovanni collapsed. "I fear I am dying."

"Giovanni!" Brother Francis cried in alarm. Kneeling by the man he whispered, "Wait! Listen. We will pray. Giovanni, God will give us water. His mercy . . ."

Giovanni's gasps rattled in his dry throat. His eyes rolled back in his head. He could not answer.

Brother Francis clasped his hands and began to beseech God in prayer. After several moments, Brother Francis stretched his hands toward heaven. "Heavenly Father, you who bring rain to fill the lakes and rivers, hear our prayer. You who breathe the dew upon the face of the dawn, we beg you, hear our prayer. You who sent your son in water and in blood, send us water to help this suffering soul. I know how tender you are to all who love you. Giovanni loves you. I love you with all my heart. Have mercy on us. Send us living water that we may live to bring you glory!"

Giovanni found himself listening and watching. Even in his suffering, he marveled at the persistence of the little poor man.

As Giovanni watched, Brother Francis' face shone with joy, his words tumbling out like water from a sudden spring:

"Lord Jesus, Son of the living God, glory of heaven and earth,
have mercy on us.

Lord Jesus, Son of the living God, giver of all good things,
have mercy on us.

Lord Jesus, Son of the living God, strength of the weak,
have mercy on us.

Lord Jesus, Son of the living God, consoler of the dying,
have mercy on us.

Lord Jesus, Son of the living God, filling men with hope,
have mercy on us.

Lord Jesus, Son of the living God, builder of our faith,
have mercy on us.

Lord Jesus, Son of the living God, source of all love,
have mercy on us.

Lord Jesus, Son of the living God, incarnation of mercy,
have mercy on us . . ."

So the litany of praise rolled like sweet music from Brother Francis' thin lips, astounding Giovanni.

As Francis was praying, Giovanni began to say the response, "have mercy on us," with him.

Suddenly, Brother Francis dropped his arms and opened his eyes wide!

"Quickly, get up, Giovanni!" Brother Francis cried.

Before the peasant could protest that he was far too weak, Brother Francis pulled him to his feet. "Hurry . . . over there." Pointing to a tall boulder a few steps away, Brother Francis rushed to it with him. "Jesus Christ, our Lord, has opened the font of his mercy! He has brought living water from the rock to quench your thirst!"

Stumbling, Giovanni's eyes opened wider and wider. Out of the rock a great gushing torrent of water sprayed. Ducking his head into it, he drank and drank and drank.

Brother Francis brought the donkey so that it, too, could drink. "Never be forgetful of God's little creatures," he said softly.

Once they had finished, Brother Francis climbed back up on the donkey. "Let us go now, if your thirst is quenched."

Slowly, Giovanni got to his feet. Taking the reins he began up the mountain. Every once in a while he glanced back. Before they rounded the curve in the path, the flow of water from the tall boulder had stopped.

"It was . . . a miracle," Giovanni whispered, more to himself than to Brother Francis. Looking up at the little poor man, he silently marveled that God used him in so wondrous a way. So thin, so weary, so sick and, yet, Giovanni felt the joy radiating from Brother Francis as he gave thanks.

Suddenly Giovanni was ashamed. So very ashamed of

all the things he had been thinking of the poor little brother. 'So the stories are true,' he thought. 'This little brother of Assisi is a great lover of God, and God of him. And all those stories, the ones of his love of poverty, of his holiness and love of creation, they are not exaggerated.' Giovanni bowed his head and silently begged the Lord to forgive him for doubting his little poor man.

Finally, they arrived at the hermitage. Giovanni helped Brother Francis down, saying, "Here we are."

"How wonderful. You were right, Giovanni, it was a hard climb!" Brother Francis said, beaming at the peasant man. "I am so glad you let me ride your donkey. Thank you."

"Here," Giovanni said suddenly, "take this food. It will feed you for at least a week." Shoving the sack of food he had planned to consume on his way down the mountain at Brother Francis, he grinned.

"Oh! Thank you," Brother Francis bowed his head humbly, "but I do not deserve this good abundance, as I rode the donkey. You need the food. You walked all the way, Giovanni."

"No, no," Giovanni held up his hand stubbornly. "I am going to fast all the way back down the mountain. I will offer my fast as a gift of thanksgiving for the blessed miracle of God's mercy."

"What a marvelous thank-you offering," Brother Francis said. "Surely I shall fast with you!" Smiling, he added, "And if you meet some poor pilgrim or beggar on the way home, offer this abundance of food to them for the love of Jesus!"

Giovanni laughed. "Very well," he said. "I will do it!"

As Giovanni left, a great feeling of peace descended on him. 'God treats all men alike,' he thought. 'If they love him, they are treated as his beloved sons.'

Thus Giovanni traveled all the way down the mountain thanking the Lord in his heart. As he passed the tall rock where the living water had flowed forth, he marveled that it was again as dry as desert sand.

'Brother Francis can truly teach us how to love Jesus,' Giovanni thought, remembering the spontaneous litany of mercy. Whenever he took pilgrims up the mountain thereafter, he would tell them how God had mercy on a thirsty peasant through the prayers of one little brother from Assisi.

John was a

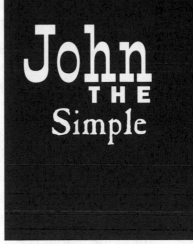

John THE Simple

very simple man. Large of body and strong as an ox, he could do the work of ten men. Because of this, his parents did not mind that he was like an innocent child. He could never grasp difficult things but gave up quickly or came to some conclusion of his own. Instead of learning difficult things he did what he knew—

farming, ploughing, shoveling and cleaning. He did all of this very well.

Although he was simple, he had a secret wish. That wish was that someday somehow he would be able to serve the Lord.

One day as he was eating with his parents and younger brother, he heard something that interested him very much. He even stopped eating to listen.

"Some of those brothers are in town," his younger brother said, tearing off a hunk of bread and handing it to John.

"Ah, yes. I am surprised the people let those beggars back into Assisi," his father said, passing a piece of cheese to John and motioning him to keep eating.

"They were working at the farm across from us some days ago," his brother grunted, chewing his food noisily.

"Working!" John's mother laughed. "I thought they were beggars. That's what I heard."

"They will work for food," the brother said. "One of the men told me they are serving God in a new way."

"It's a new way, all right," the father chuckled. "They have nothing, they live nowhere and they are going nowhere."

"Except maybe to heaven," John said thoughtfully, finally starting to eat again.

Everyone became quiet at the table, all of them staring at John. But he did not seem to notice.

John was quiet, too, but it wasn't because he was embarrassed. He was thinking about his secret. Would the new way of serving God be a way he could serve God? He knew he could not be a priest, and he was too poor to go to any of the religious groups of the times. But the new way . . . How hard could it be to have nothing, live nowhere and head for heaven?

The next day, John the Simple was ploughing the field. He moved easily behind the oxen because he was so big. He did not struggle too much like his brother did. As he guided the plough, he glanced up. In the distance he saw several figures coming toward him on the road. To his surprise, when they were close enough to identify, he saw that one of them was Brother Francis and there were several of his companions with him. John recognized them from descriptions his brother had shared at the table.

"Brothers!" John dropped the straps to the oxen and waved both hands high in the air. Crossing the field, he hurried to meet them on the road.

Brother Francis stopped. As John approached, he smiled, saying, "The peace of the Lord Jesus be upon you!"

"And with you!" John cried at once, making the Sign of the Cross slowly and reverently. "I stopped you because I would like you to make me a brother." He looked hopefully at Brother Francis. "I have long wanted to serve God." Turning to look at each of their faces, John bowed his head to wait for an answer. Then raising his brows, he looked up and said to Brother Francis, "I will live without anything. I will have no home, and I will go with you as a companion on your journey to heaven."

"What is your name?" Brother Francis asked gently.

"John," the man said, folding his calloused hands, "John the Simple, my parents call me."

"What joy there must be in heaven," Brother Francis said at once. His eyes alight with happiness. He turned to each of the brothers and said, "For this man thinks nothing of himself and wants to give everything up to serve God." Turning back to John he said, "If, brother, you want to become our companion, give all you have to the poor. Then I will receive you and we will continue our journey to heaven!"

For a moment, John just stood staring. As he thought about what Brother Francis said, a smile spread over his face. Then hurrying back to the oxen, he unhitched one. "Here, little brothers. Let us give this ox to the poor. I deserve to receive that much from my father's goods after all the years I have worked."

Brother Francis smiled.

"I will take off my clothes and go with you naked. That way I will have something else to give to the poor and I will have given all that I have." John immediately began to take off his shirt.

At that moment his father saw him. "John, John, what are you doing?" he yelled, hurrying from the house toward his large son.

"It looks like he is giving those beggars his clothes!" John's younger brother said, running next to their father toward John.

"Stop, John!" the father panted to a halt, staring first at one brother then the other. "Why are you taking off your shirt?"

"I am going naked with these brothers to serve God.

We shall give my clothes and this ox to the poor. Then I will have given everything away!" John smiled down at his father.

"The ox! You are taking the ox?" his father cried, his face getting redder and redder.

For a moment there was a little arrow of sadness in Brother Francis' heart, because he could see the father cared more for the ox than his own son.

"You can't take that ox!" the younger brother cried. "It is too hard to plough with just one. I would be exhausted!"

John's mother hurried to join them. "No, you cannot take the ox. We need it to plough the fields. It is not yours, John," his mother said angrily.

"But surely I deserve one ox," John said gently, not at all deterred from his purpose.

"The ox! You would take one of the team and leave us without?" they complained loudly.

"Stop!" Brother Francis held his hands up. "Be of easy minds." Placing a thin hand on the ox, Brother Francis looked into the father's eyes. "Behold," he said firmly, "I give you the ox and take your son." Taking John's arm he guided him away.

Neither father, mother nor younger brother protested. John the Simple was not as valuable to them as their team of oxen.

"Come, John," Brother Francis said cheerfully. "We shall be your family. You shall be my special companion."

John the Simple smiled the smile of an angel. His secret wish was beginning.

As they walked toward home, Brother Francis spoke of the grace of simplicity to encourage John the Simple not to be sad because he saw that he was different from others.

"Yes. It is true that you are different. But you are

different in a wonderful way."

John grinned sheepishly, but his eyes said he was eager to hear Brother Francis' words.

"The Lord Jesus has given you the special gift of simplicity, and that gift is something most grown men and women do not have." Brother Francis' eyes reflected all the joy he felt at speaking of God's gifts. "With simplicity, a man sees things as they are. He does not pretend they are one way or another to please himself or others. They are as they are." Nodding at John, he went on, "With simplicity, right is right and wrong is wrong. There is no argument that something may be a little wrong." Smiling, he saw John nod very seriously. "With simplicity a man does not justify his words or actions. He says or does them out of uncomplicated motives—because he wants to. Or because he doesn't want to, in the case of not doing some things."

"What does all that mean?" John the Simple asked.

Cocking his head, Brother Francis could not help smiling. "It means that the simpler your life is, the more you are able to love God above all things and do his will unselfishly."

So Brother Francis received John the Simple into the brotherhood. Everyone found him refreshing and a very good example because he took all his instructions to heart and worked at his tasks with all that he was and had.

Brother Francis often had cause to smile at John's simplicity. Sometimes when Brother Francis would stand in one place to meditate, John would stand still, too! Whatever gestures or movements Brother Francis made, John the Simple made, too. If Brother Francis spat, John the Simple spat. If Brother Francis coughed, John the Simple coughed. If Brother Francis sniffed, John the

Simple sniffed. If he folded his hands, John folded his hands.

John the Simple even joined his sighs to Brother Francis' sighs. If Brother Francis wept, John would weep, also. When Brother Francis raised his hands to heaven, John the Simple raised his as well. John seemed to watch Brother Francis diligently, copying everything he did.

One day, Brother Francis saw John copying him.

"John, why do you imitate me?" Brother Francis asked, full of curiosity.

"Because," John answered immediately, "I promised myself I would do everything you do so I, too, could be holy." John lowered his heavy brows very seriously. "It could be dangerous to my soul to omit anything," he explained.

"What wonderful simplicity!" Brother Francis said to himself, "wanting to imitate one's superiors in everything, in order to strive to be holy."

But to Brother John the Simple, Francis said, "You must not do everything I do." Brother Francis was very careful to be gentle so as not to hurt John. "You see, John, the good Lord leads each of us down a unique road, a path. He gives to each only one. So if you copy me, you will be neglecting the path he has chosen for you."

"I see," Brother John said soberly. "Very well, I shall only do the things I know will please God!"

"Wonderful!" Brother Francis cried. "Let all the brothers copy Brother John the Simple in that one perfect thing. Let them do only what they know will please God. Then all will go according to the perfect will of God!"

Brother John smiled, his eyes gentle with thought. "Yes," he said slowly, "and God will be glorified."

"Amen," Brother Francis said, taking the big man's

hand. "Now let us go and pray, for prayer always pleases the Good Lord."

John the Simple stayed with the brothers until his death. Thereafter, Brother Francis called him Saint John the Simple, when he spoke of him to others.

Why?

"Because," he said thoughtfully, "simplicity accompanies holiness in life. And holiness opens the door to heaven."

"Looooook!"

THE Money Snake

Brother Borgus drew the word out until he ran out of air. His eyes popped open. Pointing, he shot a quick look at Brother Francis. He was still walking down the road to Apulia. They were on a pilgrimage.

"What is it?" Brother Francis craned his neck, his dark eyes flashing curiosity.

"It is a purse, a very large purse," Brother Borgus said, awe making his voice quiver.

"A purse?" Squinting his eyes, Brother Francis stared at the large lump gleaming in the road.

"And it is bursting with money!" Brother Borgus almost panted.

"Ah, money." Raising his eyebrows and nodding, Brother Francis sighed. "Yes, it does seem to have split open. Too much money for such a small sack."

Brother Borgus turned, staring at Brother Francis. "What a gift we can give to the poor!" he said with a delighted grin.

"Oh, no." Brother Francis shook his head and kept walking.

"Dear Brother," Brother Borgus sputtered, staring at the bag and then at Brother Francis' retreating form, "we ought to pick it up."

Brother Francis didn't answer. Walking slowly, he motioned with one hand that his companion should hurry and join him.

The shuffling thump of Brother Borgus's sandaled feet was loud in the morning air. As soon as Brother Borgus was beside him, Brother Francis said, "Don't you see, dear Brother? That money purse, bursting with coins, is a trick of the devil."

"A trick of the devil!" Brother Borgus blustered. "All that money will relieve hundreds of poor people suffering want, who are starving, exposed to the elements, hated and outcast."

"Stop, stop, stop," Brother Francis chuckled. But then he grew very serious. "The money in itself could do great and worthwhile things."

"So why don't we go back and get it?" Brother Borgus interrupted, stopping in his tracks. Folding his arms across his barrel chest he waited.

"Because it belongs to someone else," Brother Francis said gently. "It would be a sin to make a gift of something to someone, if the gift did not belong to you in the first place."

"But . . ."

"It is not ours to give," Brother Francis cut him off. His voice had a firm edge in it.

Brother Borgus compressed his thick lips, finally silent. But it was easy to see he was troubled by the thought of leaving the brimming money sack behind.

Picking up their pace, they traveled for an hour without speaking about it. At last, Brother Borgus could keep to himself no longer.

"I can't help thinking how hard you have gotten to the needs of the poor," Brother Borgus mused aloud. Knowing Brother Francis welcomed speaking any kind of criticism, Brother Borgus knew Brother Francis would listen humbly. So Brother Borgus went on, "So many coins would feed children, infants, whole families. It would help those, who at this very moment, are suffering the agony of empty bellies." He snuffled, his eyes brimming. "Many of them have no hope for relief."

Saying nothing, Brother Francis continued to walk. Brother Borgus hurried to catch up. "Listen," he said suddenly, "up ahead there is a family camping by the road. Let us ask them what they would do if they found a money sack."

Brother Francis' face brightened at this, for he loved any opportunity to share with others, especially if the sharing was about God and God's laws. "Yes, let us ask them," he said.

Before Brother Borgus could speak, the little brother hurried to the fire. "Peace be upon you in the holy name of Jesus," he said.

"And peace be upon you," the man smiled, motioning the two brothers to join them and eat with them.

"How kind of you to ask us to share, but we are on a journey and cannot spare the time," Brother Francis smiled apologetically. "But if it is all right, may I ask you a question which my good brother and I have been speaking about but have not agreed on the answer?"

Exchanging puzzled looks with his wife, the man smiled too, "Of course, little Brother. If I can help, I will be blessed to do so."

"Very well," Brother Francis said, folding his hands and lowering his chin. After Brother Borgus was beside him, he spoke. "If you lost your money purse on the road, would you feel the man who found it had merit if he gave all of your money away as gifts to the poor?"

Brother Borgus's eyebrows descended, his mouth bowed in a frown. "Of course not. I would go back and search for my money purse until I found it," he declared indignantly. "I would hope and pray, if someone picked it up, they would look for whoever lost it."

"I see," said Brother Francis. Turning to look evenly into Brother Borgus's eyes, his expression said, "Do you see?" To the couple he said, "Thank you, good people. And God be with you on your journey."

With that, the brothers continued their own journey. After walking for another few miles, Brother Borgus could no longer keep his thoughts to himself. So once again, he cleared his throat and spoke.

"You are without mercy, Brother Francis," Brother Borgus said soberly. "Of course those people would be eager to have their own money purse back. But what of the poor? Did they give one thought to all the good that can be done with the lost money?"

Brother Francis sighed. Glancing worriedly at Brother Borgus, he thought, 'He is deceived by a spirit of false generosity.' But he said, "Brother Borgus, do not be deceived by false generosity. The devil will try in any way he can to get us to sin. And to give the possessions of another away without their consent is a sin."

"A sin," Brother Borgus grunted, his cheeks flaming red. "False generosity." Shaking his head he stopped walking. Putting his hands on his hips he said, "I will have no peace thinking of the suffering that will go on because we did not pick up that purse!"

"What purse?" Quite unexpectedly, a tall man stepped from the shadows of the afternoon sun.

"The lost purse on the road," Brother Borgus said, stepping back from the man. His worried eyes clearly saying, "Where did you come from?" There had been no one in front of them and no one behind them.

"Maybe I can help," the man said, a slow charming smile spreading across his face. "You brothers are having an argument. Maybe I can solve it for you."

Brother Francis studied the tall man, his inky black eyes reflecting the cunning he saw in the other man back to him. But the little brother did not comment. Instead he turned to Brother Borgus.

"Let us return to the purse, good Brother," said Francis, "for God knows I do not want you to have turmoil in your heart and soul."

With a bright smile, Brother Borgus nodded. Then, scratching his thick beard he began to tell the stranger about the bulging sack of money.

All the while they walked and walked and walked. Passing the little family, Brother Francis waved. On down the long road early into evening they walked. Finally they turned the corner. A few yards away the bulge of the money sack made a black blot on the road.

"So, that is what we would be able to do with such a great quantity of money," Brother Borgus huffed. He had been telling the tall man all about the worthy deeds that could be accomplished with the lucky find.

"An admirable end for a lost sack of money," the stranger agreed. His eyes seemed to dance with a delighted fire.

But Brother Francis did not smile. His thin lips moved in prayer. He watched the stranger with steely reserve that was quite outside his generous and gentle character.

Brother Borgus noticed Francis' expression. He stopped speaking and looked at his companion uncomfortably. "Well, here we are," he said uneasily.

"Yes," Brother Francis said, making the Sign of the Cross, "here we are."

Licking his lips, Brother Borgus waited, unsure of what he should do.

At last, Brother Francis spoke, his voice very soft and kind, "Go, dear Brother, and pick up the purse."

Brother Borgus shuddered. The power in the little brother's voice made goose bumps come up on his arms and neck. Glancing at the stranger, Brother Borgus noticed that the man had moved away from Brother Francis.

"Do not be afraid," Brother Francis said, pulling his attention back to the purse. "We are here to unmask the devil's trickery!"

The tall stranger laughed very softly, but he did not come any closer to the two brothers. He moved nearer to the bag.

"The de . . . devil," Brother Borgus stuttered, fear making his voice quake.

"Go, pick up the bag," Brother Francis urged.

Brother Borgus drew a long determined breath. He could feel the power of Brother Francis' prayers. It was like a light flowing forth from him and over Brother Borgus. And he saw the darkness around the stranger. Yet, still the money spilled from the bag, gleaming tantalizingly.

"You can do so much good," the stranger said, his smile spreading snake-like across his dark features.

Brother Borgus made the Sign of the Cross. Stepping forward he reached for the bag. As his hand descended, a huge snake lunged out of the bag to strike him! But it could not. It writhed for a few seconds in the light surrounding the brother's hand and disappeared in a hiss of smoke. Moments later a great cloud of smoke enveloped the stranger and the gleaming sack, and they were gone!

Whirling, Brother Borgus cried, "I am a blind fool, Brother Francis!" Tears streaming down his cheeks, he clasped his hands and went on, "I would have fallen into a terrible sin by the trickery of the devil!"

Hurrying to Brother Borgus, Brother Francis' compassion overcame him. Throwing his arms around him, Francis comforted him, saying, "It is over, dear Brother, it is over."

Brother Borgus shook for some time, fear and relief fighting for release.

"Try and remember, my brother," Brother Francis said gently, "the end never justifies the means." Then turning to look back where the money bag had been, he said, "No one can do evil and achieve good. Evil brings evil. Good deeds bring good results. The good tree cannot give us bad fruit, just as the evil or bad tree cannot give good fruit."

Brother Borgus shuddered. "Forgive me," he said.

"God forgives all sinners whose hearts are filled with true sorrow," said Francis. Assuring him with a smile that he held no bad feelings, he said, "Come. Let us finish our journey, rejoicing in all the Lord has shown us."

"Yes, my brother," Brother Borgus returned very humbly, "I shall never never forget this lesson. It has taught me that the love of money truly is the very root of all the evils in this world."

"Indeed," Brother Francis agreed soberly, "the love of money is a poisonous snake to the virtues of the soul. Truly it is a tool of the devil."

And so the enemy's treacherous cunning had been unmasked before the eyes of Brother Borgus, revealed and defeated by the love of poverty and the power of prayer, all through the humble hands of the little poor man of Assisi, Brother Francis.

"What is

MIRACLES of the Manger

Brother Francis' greatest intention?" Brother Arturo grunted, shoveling manure from the stable.

"What do you mean?" Brother Zachary asked, wiping perspiration from his eyes.

"You have been one of his companions for many years. What is his chief desire?" Brother Arturo asked, digging his shovel into the heap of dung and leaning on it.

"To follow, to live the holy gospel of Jesus Christ in all things, of course."

"So, it is also our desire," said Brother Arturo. "The difference is his zeal and determination. He does everything as if a fire were burning in him. He lives with the full attention of his heart, his soul and his mind. I guess I would say, he is trying to do what the Lord Jesus would do and say, and live his commandments."

"Yes, when I think of how he lives I am inspired. But at times I wonder if I am fit for this life. Especially when I compare my efforts to his," Brother Zachary said, a little dejected.

Brother Arturo did not comment for three shovelfuls of manure. Then he said, "We cannot compare ourselves to him, but we should try our best to do as he does. Just as he recalls and tries to do as the Lord Jesus Christ did."

Brother Zachary shoveled harder, trying to ignore the chill in his toes. He wasn't sure he felt better after what Brother Arturo said. He wanted to be like Brother Francis.

"In a few weeks it will be Christmas," Brother Arturo huffed. "Do you remember the event in our Lord's life Brother Francis speaks about frequently?"

"I would say the Incarnation." Brother Zachary smiled at the thought. "If Brother Francis had his way, he would recreate the very manger our Lord was born in, just to kindle devotion to his birth."

Brother Arturo nodded, "Yes. He speaks so much of the Lord's birth, it astounds me."

"That and the Lord's passion," Brother Zachary said. Then, wiggling his toes against the cold, he said, "But Christmas is my most favorite time. It is like the beginning of the Passion, in a way."

Brother Arturo looked at him for a long moment, but before he could speak, another brother hurried in.

"Do either of you know why Brother Francis sent for John?" the brother asked.

Both Arturo and Zachary shook their heads.

"You mean, Noble John?" Brother Arturo asked.

"Yes, yes, that John. He is always sending for him for one reason or another. But this time," the brother rolled his shoulders, as if trying to unseat a shudder, "I feel that something special is up." Looking at each of the brothers he went on, "You know how excited Brother Francis gets at Christmas."

Again the brothers nodded. Together they hurried out of the stable and back to the main house where the brothers lived at Greccio. As they came in, they heard Brother Francis talking to John. All of them knew how much the little poor man respected the one they called John the Noble. The man was reputed to pursue the virtues of the soul so persistently that even Brother Francis was amazed.

"So, if you desire to celebrate the Lord's birth in Greccio, go quickly and do all those things I have told you," Brother Francis was saying.

"Yes, I will, dear Brother," they heard John the Noble say.

"Because I hope to do something this year that will be very special, by the grace of God. I want to make everyone remember how the Lord Jesus became a humble little infant." Brother Francis' voice was filled with awe. "I want people to realize the inconveniences, the hardships of his infant needs. I want them to see with their eyes how he lay in a chilly manger with a lowly ox and ass standing by. How he lay where he was put, so helpless, so vulnerable, yet with such beauty and majesty people came to worship him, recognizing his divinity, even in such a humble form."

The brothers listening could almost see the glowing face of Brother Francis as they heard his words.

"Don't worry, I will take care of everything," John the Noble answered. Then the approach of his feet sounded louder.

The brothers turned away, trying to look busy outside the door. One began to clean the table. One took a broom from the corner and began to sweep and the last sat quickly on a chair and cradled his beads, beginning to pray.

John the Noble hurried through, glancing neither to the left nor to the right. The brothers exchanged wondering looks.

Brother Francis burst out of the inner room. "Brothers, Greccio shall soon be a new Bethlehem!" he exclaimed.

Speechless, they all froze, staring.

"Brother Arturo, go to the men and women of Greccio and tell them that on the eve of the Nativity to come to John the Noble's stable in the woods. Come carrying candles or lanterns to light up the night, just as the Star of Bethlehem lit the night so long ago."

"Yes, Brother," Brother Arturo said and rushed from the room, dropping the broom.

"Brother Zachary, go and beg extra hay for John the

Noble's stable. Beg extra feed. Beg a trough to give the animals water and food." Then pausing, Francis' eyes grew wide, like a dark shining night sky. Pinpoints of light gleamed in the pupils. "Finally, beg a small cradle."

"Yes, Brother," Brother Zachary cried, setting the cups back on the table and rushing out.

"Brother Domino, go to the priest and beg him, for the love of Jesus, to come on the eve of Christmas and say the holy Mass for all of the people, at John the Noble's stable."

"Yes, Brother Francis." Brother Domino also rushed out to obey.

The weeks passed quickly. Brother Arturo, Brother Zachary and Brother Domino accomplished their tasks and returned with amazement to their house.

The holy night arrived. Brother Francis called all the brothers to go with him to the stable in the woods.

Slowly the brothers made their way through the darkened trees. The ground crackled with cold. Their breath came in white puffs. Their noses and ears tingled as the chill of the night settled around them. Their candles flickered in the darkness. Each little halo lit up reddened cheeks. Each candle revealed faces glowing with expectation. As the brothers walked, people from the village joined them, carrying candles and lanterns.

Brother Francis lifted his voice as they walked. As he sang, the sound carried through the dark woods. The praises of the birth of Jesus filled the night with a strange sense that something was about to happen. One by one the people joined their voices to the little brother's.

The sound swelled, rippling through the trees. As the people came to a clearing, Brother Francis stepped forward, his eyes full of love.

"Behold, good people," he said, "the lowly stable where

the Son of God began his pilgrimage to save our souls." Kneeling, Francis bowed his head.

The people shuffled to a stop. Staring in wonder, they saw the crude stable, the rough wood barely keeping out the chill of the winter air. They saw the ox and the ass and the sheep huddled close by. Hay was spread inside the stable, looking like gold against the darkness.

And in the front sat a crib, carved from dark wood, filled with straw, waiting. The people began to kneel.

"Here in a stable with nothing but his swaddling clothes the King of Heaven breathed his first breaths as a God-man." Brother Francis' voice quivered with exaltation, as he honored the simplicity of Christ's birth.

"Amen," the people breathed, almost as one.

"Here, rejected by all others, with only the love of Mother Mary and her spouse, blessed Joseph, our Infant King revealed that the love of heaven is the greater treasure, even greater than all the riches of men," Brother Francis said, exalting our Lord Jesus' poverty.

"Amen," the people sighed, again as one voice.

"Here," Brother Francis called out, "the King of Glory lay, unable to care for his least needs, but he was satisfied to be nurtured by the hands of those who could barely understand his majesty." Brother Francis inhaled slowly, trembling as he commended the awesome nature of the Lord's humility.

"Amen," the people cried, and the night was lit up like day by their candles and by their joy.

The priest came forward and celebrated the Holy Mass over the manger. His face seemed to glow with devotion. People exclaimed with wonder, for many of them knew this priest had nearly lost confidence in his faith. But that night his consolation was like a new garment clothing his soul.

After the Mass, Brother Francis turned to speak to the people.

"All of us know the story of the Holy Nativity," he began, "but how many of us understand its purpose?" Looking from face to face, he was filled with a great sweetness, seeing the hope and expectation in the peoples' eyes.

"We know Christ came in poverty," Francis continued, "so we will understand that attachment to this world is vain. So we will see the greatness of heaven and its treasures. So we will realize we are pilgrims who come into this world with nothing. We come for one purpose; to love him and attain heaven." He saw nodding heads and smiles.

"We also know," Francis said, "that our Lord's humbleness was the measure of his glory, because taking the most vulnerable form, he showed us we have no power. We, too, must humble ourselves to gain goodness, and not to think we are good, for we are sinners, while he had no sin. But the thing we miss, when we look into the stable and see the vision of a babe in the crib, is the suffering, the bitter chill of winter, the hurt of rejection, the sorrow of having so little. We do not see these things. We must look at them. We must see that they remind us that he was obedient to the will of the Father."

The word obedience was a harsh word to the ears of most people, so Brother Francis spoke it softly, and, lifting his eyes to heaven, he went on without looking into the faces of the people, "Through his humble obedience, the Passion began. Good people, the Incarnation of our Lord, is the heartbeat of his Passion and suffering. Just as all babes are born to die, Christ Jesus was born to suffer, die and rise so that we may live. In the chill of his birth, he felt the fire of sorrow for sin—our sins. He is God and knows and knew his purpose before all time began. The Birth and the Passion are one—the bloodless and the bloody sacrifices. For that is what the Nativity is, the beginning of the sacrifice of sufferings for us."

As Francis looked again into the faces of the people, he saw wonder there, eyes glowing like the candles they held. A new joy was kindled in the hearts of the people for the holy infant Jesus. Greccio had truly become a New Bethlehem.

Brother Francis walked slowly to the manger and placed a babe in the straw. Though it was made of finely painted clay, some thought the infant smiled and stretched out arms to the people, as if Brother Francis had awakened the baby from a deep, deep sleep. The infant reached out to the crowd beseechingly. Struck silent, awe settled over the souls of the people.

Then softly, softly, they began to sing a melodious Christmas lullaby, as if the clay babe were truly Christ in the lowly manger. Brother Francis wept for joy.

Finally, the solemn celebration ended. All of the people returned to their homes, each heart trembling with a new awareness of the gift of the Holy Nativity.

The hay of the manger was distributed to the people as they left. Even the brothers took some with them. Brother Arturo took a bunch with him and stored it in the stable.

"Why are you saving that hay?" Brother Zachary asked one day, a week after the holy night.

"I think," Brother Arturo dropped his voice to a whisper, "I think, with the holiness of that night, I mean the presence of the Lord . . ." Unable to put it into words, he shrugged, then he blurted out, "I have given it to the sick cow. She had stopped giving milk. She is dying."

Brother Zachary looked puzzled. "The brown cow?" he asked.

"Yes," answered Brother Arturo, "the brown cow."

"But I just milked her," said Brother Zachary, "she doesn't seem ill!"

Brother Arturo cried out with joy. Running to the cow's stall, he stared. To his astonishment, Brother Zachary was right. The cow had been completely cured!

"God be praised!" Brother Arturo shouted. The two brothers danced a jig of joy.

Several days passed.

"How many have you counted?" Brother Zachary whispered to Brother Arturo. The crackling of the fire grew louder as Brother Arturo looked around to see if anyone else were listening.

"Several women were relieved of horrible struggles to bear children. That makes six miracles and fifty people that have been cured of illnesses the doctors said were hopeless, both men and women."

"And many we don't know about. Just by touching the hay," Brother Zachary said in amazement, forgetting to whisper.

"Yes, just by touching the hay from the first manger," Brother Arturo breathed loudly. For a long time his eyes were misty with tears. "Everyone everywhere should build a manger on the Holy Nativity."

"Surely, I agree," Brother Francis said, joining them by the fire. "Miracles come when the heart of Jesus rejoices at the tender love of man for their God. When we love him, we bring his marvelous mercy into our lives. That is the true miracle of the manger."

"Amen," the brothers said.

"Amen," blessed Brother Francis echoed, bowing his head in a prayer of thanksgiving. Silently he promised himself to have a manger every year at Greccio, and all the other houses in which his little brothers lived!